100 Questions (and Answers) About Qualitative Research

Q&A SAGE 100 Questions and Answers Series

Neil J. Salkind, Series Editor

1. *100 Questions (and Answers) About Research Methods*, by Neil J. Salkind

2. *100 Questions (and Answers) About Tests and Measurement*, by Bruce B. Frey

3. *100 Questions (and Answers) About Statistics*, by Neil J. Salkind

4. *100 Questions (and Answers) About Qualitative Research* by Lisa M. Given

Visit **sagepub.com/100qa** for a current listing of titles in this series.

100 Questions (and Answers) About Qualitative Research

Lisa M. Given

Charles Sturt University

Los Angeles | London | New Delhi
Singapore | Washington DC | Boston

Los Angeles | London | New Delhi
Singapore | Washington DC | Boston

FOR INFORMATION:

SAGE Publications, Inc.
2455 Teller Road
Thousand Oaks, California 91320
E-mail: order@sagepub.com

SAGE Publications Ltd.
1 Oliver's Yard
55 City Road
London EC1Y 1SP
United Kingdom

SAGE Publications India Pvt. Ltd.
B 1/I 1 Mohan Cooperative Industrial
Area
Mathura Road, New Delhi 110 044
India

SAGE Publications Asia-Pacific Pte.
Ltd.
3 Church Street
#10–04 Samsung Hub
Singapore 049483

Acquisitions Editor: Vicki Knight
Associate Editor: Katie Guarino
Editorial Assistant: Yvonne McDuffee
Production Editor: Libby Larson
Copy Editor: Amy Rosenstein
Typesetter: C&M Digitals (P) Ltd.
Proofreader: Kate Macomber Stern
Indexer: Pilar Wyman
Cover Designer: Candice Harman
Marketing Manager: Nicole Elliott

Copyright © 2016 by SAGE Publications, Inc.

Printed in the United States of America

Library of Congress Cataloging-in-Publication Data

Given, Lisa M.

100 questions (and answers) about qualitative research / Lisa M. Given.

pages cm
Includes bibliographical references and index.

ISBN 978-1-4833-4564-2 (pbk. : alk. paper)

1.Qualitative research—Methodology. 2. Social sciences—Research—Methodology. I. Title. II. Title: One hundred questions (and answers) about qualitative research.

H62.G5166 2016
001.4'2—dc23   2014047615

This book is printed on acid-free paper.

SFI® Certified Sourcing
www.sfiprogram.org
SFI-00453

15 16 17 18 19 10 9 8 7 6 5 4 3 2 1

Contents

SAGE was founded in 1965 by Sara Miller McCune to support the dissemination of usable knowledge by publishing innovative and high-quality research and teaching content. Today, we publish more than 750 journals, including those of more than 300 learned societies, more than 800 new books per year, and a growing range of library products including archives, data, case studies, reports, conference highlights, and video. SAGE remains majority-owned by our founder, and after Sara's lifetime will become owned by a charitable trust that secures our continued independence.

Los Angeles | London | Washington DC | New Delhi | Singapore | Boston

Preface

Like all research approaches, qualitative research offers a complex and varied way to understand the world around us. Although many people learn the craft of qualitative research during years of advanced education (such as completing a PhD), others come to qualitative work from quantitative backgrounds, particularly those wanting to use mixed-methods designs in their work. Researchers and students in all disciplines—from health to social sciences, and even the fine arts—are finding that qualitative approaches are a great fit to understand people's views and experiences.

100 Questions (and Answers) About Qualitative Research addresses some of the most common questions asked by new and more senior qualitative researchers. Members of mixed-methods' teams, supervisors, research assistants, students, practitioner-researchers, and others can use this book as a quick reference to the key issues that come up in qualitative design. The intention is to outline some of the core, fundamental topics that shape the practice of qualitative research. When used as a supplement to other readings, this book will help readers gain a comprehensive view of qualitative inquiry. Readers who want to learn all they can about a particular methodology, setting, or research practice within a specific discipline will find many published resources to consult. This book focuses on the key, recurring questions that researchers ask when designing and implementing qualitative research. The answers are designed to cut across disciplinary and methodological lines to provide guidance on some of the most salient topics that all researchers must consider.

The questions included here are ones that I have been asked by my students, workshop attendees, practitioners, and research colleagues—across disciplines—over the years. The book is designed to serve as a companion to further study and as a place to turn first for a quick answer on a key topic. It is not meant to be an exhaustive list of questions or a comprehensive guide to all relevant answers. For those working in qualitative research already, the book may provide a refresher or a concise definition of a term for use in publications and teaching. For those new to qualitative research, the book will provide an overview of key topics, challenges, and benefits of qualitative inquiry.

The book is organized into nine parts:

- Part 1: The Nature of Qualitative Inquiry
- Part 2: Ethical Issues in Qualitative Research
- Part 3: Designing Qualitative Research
- Part 4: Ensuring Rigor in Qualitative Research Design
- Part 5: Methodologies and Methods
- Part 6: Mixed-Methods Research Involving Qualitative Approaches
- Part 7: Collecting Qualitative Data
- Part 8: Conducting Qualitative Analysis
- Part 9: Writing Qualitative Research

Each of these sections can stand alone, or the book can be read cover to cover. However, readers may also find that the questions in their minds require them to look in a few different sections. Although the book has been designed to flow from question to question, within each section, the nature of human inquiry is never linear in practice. For some readers, selecting a question in the middle of the book or reviewing the index for interesting topics may be the best way to start engaging with the content.

Each answer provided here is brief, with lists, diagrams, and tables used to highlight key points or provide examples. Although the 100 questions are designed to be independent of one another, with little overlap, there are some terms and concepts that address similar issues. A few cross-references to other questions are also provided to guide your reading of the book. The index also provides another access point for the content so that you can find your way across topics. I hope you enjoy reading it as much as I enjoyed writing it!

Acknowledgments

I would like to thank the amazing editorial and production team at Sage, and especially Vicki Knight and Libby Larson, who worked very hard to bring this book to press. A very special thanks, as well, to series editor Neil J. Salkind, who first proposed the idea for this book and then provided a great deal of support to me along the way. Thanks also to my research assistants, Rebekah Willson, Lauren Carlson, and Denise Winkler, who were always ready to brainstorm ideas when I asked, "What is the one question you wish you could ask about qualitative research?" I would also like to thank the many reviewers who provided feedback at the proposal and full manuscript stages of the writing process; their questions, critiques and guidance were invaluable in crafting the final version of this book.

And finally, thank you to my ever-supportive spouse, Dan Given, who cooked fabulous meals for us while I finished writing "just one more answer!"

SAGE Publications would like to thank the following reviewers:

- JoAnn DiGeorgio-Lutz, Texas A&M University-Commerce
- Kymberly Drawdy, Georgia Southern University
- Joe Hannah, University of Washington
- Don Haviland, California State University, Long Beach
- Christina Gringeri, University of Utah
- Shawn Long, University of North Carolina at Charlotte
- Emily Namey, FHI 360
- Michael Rosenblatt, Carleton University
- Gretchen B. Rossman, University of Massachusetts Amherst
- Johnny Saldaña, Arizona State University
- Kathleen M. Saunders, Western Washington University
- Karrie Ann Snyder, Northwestern University
- Jenny Stuber, University of North Florida

About the Author

Lisa M. Given, PhD, is Professor of Information Studies in the School of Information Studies and Associate Dean Research, Faculty of Education, at Charles Sturt University (CSU), Australia. A member of CSU's Research Institute for Professional Practice, Learning and Education, Lisa also serves as a member of the College of the Australian Research Council and is an Adjunct Professor in Humanities Computing, Faculty of Arts, and in the Faculty of Education at the University of Alberta, Canada. A former Director, and now a Distinguished Scholar, of the International Institute for Qualitative Methodology, Lisa has received numerous research grants and awards and has published widely on topics related to individuals' information behaviors, web usability, and qualitative inquiry. She has taught workshops on qualitative research methods for more than a decade and is Editor of *The Sage Encyclopedia of Qualitative Research Methods* (2008). Additional information can be found on Lisa's website at www.lisagiven.com

PART 1

THE NATURE OF
QUALITATIVE INQUIRY

What Is Qualitative Research?

Qualitative research is an interesting and engaging approach to studying the ways that people experience their world. However, describing the nature of qualitative research—briefly—can be challenging, especially when there are so many different research methodologies, methods, and settings involved in these projects. In general, qualitative research is a human-focused approach to research design, which aims to delve deeply into people's experiences, perceptions, behaviors, and beliefs. Qualitative research addresses very different questions from those explored in quantitative designs. Where quantitative studies document who, what, where, how many, and other descriptive details, qualitative research explores the *why* questions that address various phenomena. Qualitative research explores the processes at play in society, examines the meanings that individuals make of particular events, and provides a window into understanding why people do what they do and think what they think.

Quantitative and qualitative research approaches can complement each other, as is common in mixed-methods designs; however, it is important to recognize that these are very different ways of doing research and ensure that appropriate expertise is available to guide mixed-methods design. Also, although most qualitative projects involve engagement, directly, with human participants, many researchers also use various textual methodologies and methods in their studies. By examining the products of human activity (such as government policy documents, photographs, diaries, blogs, etc.), researchers can also gain insight into how people think and behave. By combining textual methods with direct, human-focused methods, researchers can gather rich, deep data about the range of human experiences in their studies.

There are a number of defining features of qualitative research, including

- A focus on people's thoughts, processes, meanings, and experiences;
- Holistic design, where actions, emotions, and beliefs are examined;

- Constructionist view of reality, where multiple meanings are possible;
- Inductive design, where theory emerges from the data;
- Emergent design, where data collection and analysis evolve as data are gathered;
- Direct researcher engagement with participants during data collection and analysis;
- Use of multiple data sources to investigate a phenomenon from various perspectives;
- Embracing of context surrounding participants' experiences;
- Acknowledgement and embracing of subjective ways of knowing;
- A focus on participants' voices in data collection, analysis, and writing; and
- An interpretive approach to data analysis and writing.

More questions? See #7, #30, and #31.

What Disciplines Use Qualitative Approaches and Are There Differences in Disciplinary Approach?

There are many different disciplines that use qualitative research. Qualitative research is very common in the social sciences, in particular, in such fields as sociology, education, social work, information science, anthropology, geography, and history. Social scientists examine the human condition in a range of settings and across various populations. The nature of human relationships, including the ways that people engage with organizations, social structures, and each other, are rich areas for analysis by qualitative researchers in these disciplines. Similarly, researchers in many health disciplines (such as nursing, public health, and medicine) also use qualitative research to understand people's experiences in health-related situations and contexts. In the arts and humanities, qualitative projects are designed to explore people's experiences of literature, drama, languages, and other fields of study. In the sciences, qualitative researchers may explore how people engage with the natural environment, how they use computer interfaces, and how simulations can enrich science classrooms. The potential for qualitative research is vast across all disciplines.

One area of innovation is in interdisciplinary research, where qualitative researchers can partner with scholars in other areas, including those who use a range of other research designs. Scholars in nursing, speech pathology, and gerontology, for example, may form research teams where qualitative methodologies are used to explore seniors' experiences of stuttering following a stroke. Education researchers may partner with physicists to use qualitative methodologies to explore first-year university students' experiences of the science classroom. Information scientists may work with computing scientists, philosophers, and linguists to conduct qualitative usability studies of online, interactive textual analysis tools. Even within a single discipline, qualitative researchers (such as social psychologists) may partner with quantitative researchers (such as clinical psychologists) to design mixed-methods projects that examine people's experiences from different perspectives.

In all of these cases, researchers' approaches to the design and implementation of qualitative studies will be shaped by their disciplinary traditions, the ways they were trained as researchers, and the influences of their academic colleagues. In the humanities, for example, researchers may use qualitative textual analysis practices rather than involving human participants in their studies, in keeping with the text-based traditions of those disciplines. In the health sciences, where clinical trials are common, qualitative researchers may conduct studies that are heavily influenced by positivist traditions in keeping with many biomedical research models. There is a spectrum of qualitative research across the disciplines, which is continually evolving as new research designs emerge and as scholars share knowledge with one another.

More questions? See #44, #97, and #98.

Is Qualitative Research Used in Practice or Only in Academic Research?

Qualitative research is often used in practice, as well as in academe. Many academic researchers work in fields with very close ties to practice, such as nursing, education, social work, business, engineering, and law. Academic projects may be designed to link the results of research directly to activities in classrooms, hospitals, corporations, and other settings. Researchers may partner with practitioners as co-investigators on a project or conduct the research in practical settings. Even where a project does not directly involve a practice setting, qualitative researchers often conduct workshops and seminars with practitioners to guide the implementation of findings into everyday practice. In some disciplines (such as medicine and information science), this is known as "evidence-based practice," which is a very deliberate approach to the use of the best available data to inform change in work environments.

Of course, there are also many "practitioner-researchers" who engage in qualitative research in their work contexts. Qualitative action research, for example, is one methodology that practitioners can use to develop projects to address specific issues in practice. However, there are a number of challenges that practitioner-researchers face in designing and implementing their own qualitative projects. Practitioner-researchers need to have various supports in place to conduct successful research projects, including

- Training and mentoring in the conduct of qualitative research, including research ethics;
- Training in the ethics review process, as many practice environments (such as schools and hospitals) require projects to go through formal ethics review;
- Financial support to fund the research (to purchase data collection equipment, to hire professional transcriptionists, etc.);

- Time to do the research (such as leave from regular duties to conduct the project); and
- Training and mentoring in the interpretation and translation of results into practice.

Many practitioners choose to partner with academic researchers to gain access to the mentoring and resources they need to conduct successful projects. These collaborations can be positive for both academics and practitioners, as each person brings unique and complementary skills to the research team. The practice context can enrich academic research, increasing the chances that the results will inform change in the workplace. In addition, the academic context can enrich practical research by ensuring that the research is of high quality and that it will be shared with other scholars and practitioners (e.g., through publications and seminars) beyond the single practice context being studied.

More questions? See #11, #44, and #97.

My Supervisor Says That Quantitative Research Is More Objective, So It's Better Than Qualitative Research. Is That True?

Qualitative research has often been criticized for being too subjective in its design. Unfortunately, this criticism demonstrates a lack of understanding about both the nature of qualitative research and the differences between subjectivity and objectivity. An objective stance is the goal in quantitative designs, where the researcher and the researched are distanced from one another. Here, the goal is to remove the influence of the researcher from the study design and implementation so that the project is valid (i.e., measures what it intends to measure), reliable (i.e., can be repeated in the future or by others, with the same results), and free from bias. For example, consider a study about the impact of government funding cuts on people with disabilities. If the government that made the cuts conducted that study, people may question the project's objectivity, particularly if the results show that the cuts had little influence on people's lives. As such positive results would benefit the government by showing that the cuts did not adversely affect people, the data would be questionable because of potential government influence in the study design. In this case, the government may hire an independent research firm to conduct the study so that the results are seen to be objective by distancing the government's researchers from the study respondents. Although it is almost impossible to design a study that is completely free from bias, there are a number of steps researchers take to ensure that biases are eliminated or (at least) managed as carefully as possible in the design and implementation of the project.

Qualitative research projects are designed to engage researchers and participants in direct ways, often for extended periods of time. These studies are grounded in a constructionist view of reality, where multiple realities exist based on people's sociocultural experiences. Qualitative researchers recognize that subjective ways of knowing are at the heart of their investigations. Objectivity is not seen as possible—or desirable—to achieve. Rather, researchers acknowledge their biases and use various strategies (such as asking neutral questions) to ensure that participants' views are at the forefront of the investigation. At the same time, qualitative researchers embrace subjectivity, as the various ways that people engage with the topic under study—including the researcher—are placed at the heart of data collection and analysis. A qualitative study of the impact of government funding cuts on people with disabilities will use various methods to explore perspectives on both (or multiple) sides of the issue; interviews with government officials and people with disabilities will be conducted to document and acknowledge the various views on the issue.

More questions? See #8, #42, and #64.

What Is the Difference Between "Ontology" and "Epistemology," and Why Do They Matter?

Ontology is the study of the nature of existence. This is a philosophical stance that explores such questions as: What does it mean to "be" in the world? What kinds of things exist around me? What is reality? For qualitative researchers working within a postmodern framework (where reality is believed to be constituted by one's history, culture, time, and place), this vision of reality allows for multiple interpretations. Here, participants in a study may explore their own perspectives about reality, which may be variable—even for those individuals who have shared a life experience or work in the same job. For qualitative researchers working within a realist framework (where a single reality is believed to exist "out there" and can be discovered in research), research projects are designed to get at the facts that shape this reality.

Epistemology explores the nature of knowledge itself. Here, a researcher might consider: How do we know what we know? What is truth? For the realist scholar, exploring the world through experimentation and the gathering of observable, empirical evidence will provide the basis for understanding the nature of knowledge. For the postmodern scholar, relative and subjective constructions of the world may also be gathered using empirical research designs; however, the meanings and intentions of these constructions are explored with the use of specific methodologies (such as critical discourse analysis) that expose the social constructions of knowledge within particular contexts.

Researchers' ontological and epistemological stances shape how researchers design and conduct their projects. The researcher's worldview shapes the decisions made about research at every stage of the project, from the types of research questions to be addressed, through the methodologies and methods chosen to gather data, as well as the presentation of results. Table 5.1 presents some key defining features of different worldviews, at different ends of a spectrum. Although researchers' worldviews are more complex than this simplified dichotomy, reviewing one's stance on these key ontological and epistemological questions can guide one's choice of an appropriate research design that will suit one's personal beliefs and understandings of the world.

Table 5.1. What's Your Worldview?

Reality Is Out There	Multiple Realities Exist
Knowledge is facts that can be gathered	Knowledge is socially constructed by people
Realist	Postmodernist
Empiricist	Constructionist
Reality is fixed	Reality is fluid
Quantitative designs	Qualitative designs
Methods designed to document facts in the world	Methods designed to critically analyze social discourses

More questions? See #8, #40, and #55.

I've Heard That Qualitative Research Is More Inductive Rather Than Deductive—What Does That Mean?

These terms—inductive and deductive—refer to the different ways that researchers engage in thinking about their data. Qualitative research is often described as inductive because theory is generated from the data gathered in the study. This is a "from-the-ground-up" approach, where research moves from the specific (data) to the general (theory) to build theory. This approach is very different from deductive studies, which take existing theories and test whether they apply to the data. Quantitative studies use a "top-down" approach, where research moves from the general (theory) to the specific (data) to test a theory.

In quantitative studies, researchers start with a theory and create a hypothesis about how they believe a phenomenon works. They gather data to test and, ideally, confirm that theory. In qualitative studies, researchers start with a research question designed to explore a phenomenon of interest. Data are gathered, initial patterns emerge, and conclusions are drawn, leading to a theory that is generated to explain the phenomenon.

Figure 6.1 Deductive (Quantitative) Research Design	**Figure 6.2** Inductive (Qualitative) Research Design

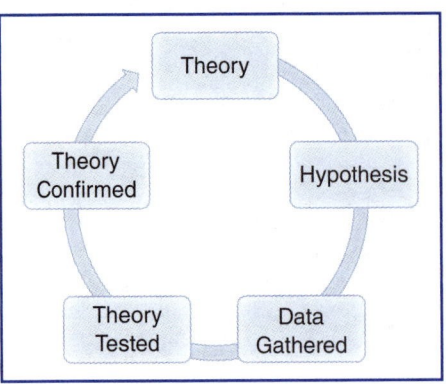
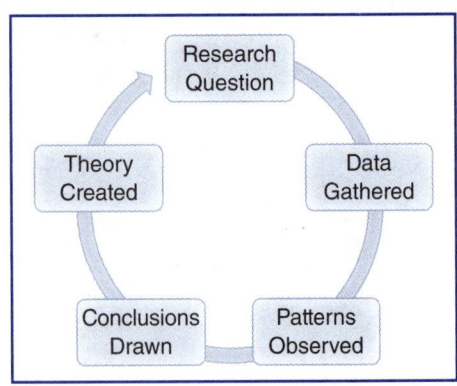

More questions? See #1, #30, and #31.

What Is the Difference Between a Project Designed With a Qualitative "Paradigm" and a Project Designed to Gather Qualitative "Data"?

A study that uses a qualitative paradigm is one that is designed to suit the inductive nature of qualitative research. The design of the study is wholly qualitative. Research questions examine people's perceptions, attitudes, and opinions, in-depth, with a focus on *why* they think as they do or *why* they act in particular ways. The methodologies and methods chosen for the study are selected to privilege participants' voices in data collection and analysis. In addition, the writing of the work is focused on providing evidence to support the interpretation of findings in participants' own words. These projects do gather qualitative data but within the context of an overarching qualitative design, and data are presented in ways that reflect the qualitative nature of the study (such as providing lengthy quotes from participant interviews or extended excerpts drawn from a qualitative content analysis).

Qualitative data can also be gathered in quantitative studies, where the overall project design does not reflect a qualitative paradigmatic approach. Open-ended questions on a quantitative questionnaire, for example, provide qualitative data but are used in ways that suit the quantitative design of the project. In these cases, the qualitative data may be examined for the frequency of particular words or analyzed to show respondents' positive or negative views on a topic. Data are often presented in tables or with brief quotes used to complement statistical analysis. Although these qualitative data provide a glimpse of participants' views on a topic, they are limited in scope and do not provide the same depth of analysis as found in studies designed with a qualitative paradigm.

One of the challenges in designing and citing mixed-methods research is understanding whether the design of the project is truly mixed or whether the project is simply using some elements of another approach. A truly mixed study reflects both quantitative and qualitative paradigms, with research designs (and research investigators) chosen to suit the nature and intent of each paradigm. These studies can be very powerful, as they will provide the best of both paradigmatic approaches, giving data that are both broad and deep, to complement each other. A quantitative design that includes some qualitative data, however, is still a quantitative design; if qualitative data are reduced to word counts and presented alongside statistical analysis, particularly if the investigators are not experts in qualitative designs, the project cannot be said to be truly mixing paradigmatic approaches. Similarly, a qualitative study that provides a count of common words used by participants is not inherently quantitative. The distinction between a qualitative paradigmatic design and one that only results in the collection of qualitative data is an important one to make.

More questions? See #1, #8, and #28.

What Is the Difference Between Quantitative Positivism and Qualitative Constructionism?

Positivism and constructionism are often positioned at opposite ends of the spectrum as to how researchers view and understand the world around them. Positivism is grounded in a realist perspective, where a single reality is believed to exist and can be measured. Universal truths are exposed through data collection and analysis using precise tests designed to deal with aggregate data. Historically, positivism is equated with quantitative research practices and the scientific method; however, many mixed-methods designs allow for a mix of quantitative/positivist investigations alongside qualitative/constructionist research. Many quantitative researchers now align their thinking with postpositivist ideals, which allow room for uncertainty and focus more on probability than a rigid belief in certain, known truths. A quantitative questionnaire, for example, may be designed to explore people's attitudes toward women's roles in society; when the questionnaire is constructed using established design principles, it can provide reliable, valid aggregate data on the issue. Some qualitative researchers also consider themselves postpositivist in their thinking, particularly those working in disciplines where the classic positivist/quantitative tradition remains the norm. In these cases, mixed-methods studies may be used, where qualitative data inform the findings of quantitative designs.

Most qualitative researchers would position themselves on the constructionist end of the reality spectrum. Constructionism is grounded in the belief that people construct reality, actively, based on how they see the world. People's understanding of reality is shaped by cultural beliefs and experiences, as well as the influence of social constructs of reality, resulting in different versions of reality for different people. Perspectives on women's roles in society, for example, will be shaped by time, geographic place, cultural understandings, social norms, and other influences on the reality of women's experiences. Qualitative researchers who are interested in studying women's role in society will aim to recruit individuals with varying perspectives in order to look for common themes across the participants. Or they may conduct research in various countries to explore the various influences that shape views on women's roles within these specific geographic areas. The goal is to give voice to the variety of people's experiences and highlight similarities and differences across participant groups. Of course, these researchers may also engage in mixed-methods research designs that incorporate quantitative data collection alongside constructionist qualitative data collection. In these cases, quantitative data may point to broad, contextual findings that can inform understandings of constructionist qualitative data.

More questions? See #5, #7, and #87.

Qualitative Research Seems to Always Involve People—Is That True?

Qualitative research is, by nature, a human-centered approach to research. For that reason, involving people as participants in the work is very common. Many research projects involve people in very direct ways, such as through interviews, focus groups, observation, and other methods of data collection designed to engage directly with participants. Researchers may talk to people, watch their activities in natural settings, ask participants to take photographs of their environments, bring groups of people together to share their views—or a mix of all of these (and other) approaches.

In other cases, research projects involve people indirectly, through the use of artifacts and texts that provide data about human experience. Researchers examine photographs, diaries, policy documents, blogs, and other materials that people have created for other purposes. These sources of data provide other ways to explore people's attitudes, opinions, and ideas, without personally talking to or engaging with participants. Often, studies involve both direct and indirect strategies as part of the triangulation process to explore phenomena from various perspectives. Direct and indirect data sources can complement and extend what a researcher will learn by using only of these approaches.

Table 9.1. Methods for Involving People in Qualitative Research—Examples

Direct Involvement	Indirect Involvement
Interviews	Blog Postings
Focus Groups	Archival Photographs
Observation	Letters to the Editor
Think-Alouds	Policy Documents
Personal Diaries	Media Reports
Photography	Twitter Archives
Etc.	Etc.

More questions? See #39, #21, and #52.

What Is the Difference Between a Research Participant and a Research Subject?

Qualitative researchers describe the people involved in their studies as *participants*, as they believe the term best captures the complexity of the research relationship. The word *subject* implies that people are, literally, the thing that is being studied—the subject or topic under investigation. As qualitative research examines processes, perceptions, and meanings related to phenomena, the term *subject* is quite limiting in its application. Similarly, the term also implies that researchers subject people to their research plans, rather than involving them in the investigation and allowing them to shape the design of the project.

The term *participant* is used to reflect people's active participation in the research. This can be a very direct level of engagement and even an ongoing process in the design (e.g., where participants are formal co-investigators in a project), or this can be an indirect and even one-time influence on the project's design (e.g., where a researcher learns something new from an interviewee and changes the interview questions asked of other participants). As qualitative research designs are emergent, evolving as the research is conducted, the role of the project's participants in that process needs to be reflected in the terms used to describe those individuals.

Despite the common use of the term *participants* by qualitative researchers, the term *human subjects* is often used as the generic term in policy documents, research ethics guidelines, and institutions. Unfortunately, this reinforces its use in other areas (e.g., journal publications), particularly in disciplines that are heavily influenced by quantitative research. In some cases, then, qualitative researchers may need to use other terms (such as *interviewees* or *respondents*) to make clear that *subjects* is not the appropriate term to represent their work. Qualitative researchers should be mindful of the implications of these terms in their own writing practices and ensure that the concept of participation is reflected in the discussion, even if the term *participants* is not used.

More questions? See #11, #72, and #91.

My Participants Are Really Co-Researchers in My Work—So What Are the Implications for My Project?

In some qualitative projects, participants work alongside the researchers as co-investigators of the phenomenon under study. Community-based participatory research, for example, is designed to have researchers and participants working in partnership. Community members and researchers work together to design the project goals, gather and analyze data, and disseminate results. Often these relationships may be ongoing, over several years, involving many different people in various roles.

There are a number of issues to consider when working with your participants as co-researchers, including

- **Ethics implications.** Researchers need to consider privacy, consent, data representation, participants' voices, dissemination, and other key ethics issues in light of the interdependent nature of researcher-participant relationships.
- **Timing implications.** Involving participants in project design means that researchers must already have established relationships with these individuals. Similarly, projects may take longer to complete, given the involvement of another group or organization in project implementation (e.g., projects may need to go through two ethics review processes, one for each organization).
- **Training implications.** Participants may need training and support in research design, ethics practices, analysis, and other research-related activities.
- **Financial implications.** Researchers and community partners may need to share costs, appropriately, depending on the nature of the project. For example, community partners may need to be compensated for time devoted to the project, or they may require special equipment to conduct the work. Similarly, researchers may need to secure partner funding from a community organization to satisfy granting agency guidelines.

- **Interpersonal implications.** Researchers and participants may be engaging in various relationships with one another—and with other, external partners—at any one time. These complex relationships require thoughtful planning in identifying and respecting the boundaries of the research project relative to other institutional outcomes.
- **Goal-setting implications.** Researchers and participants may have very different goals in mind in conducting the research. While community partners may be involved to bring about change in the organization (e.g., to satisfy a board of directors), researchers may need to disseminate results in scholarly venues that are quite removed from the local context (e.g., to satisfy tenure requirements). Balancing competing versus complementary goals is important for project success.

More questions? See #13, #83, and #100.

What Kind of Education or Training Do I Need to Conduct Qualitative Research?

Many qualitative researchers learn their craft over several years, starting with an undergraduate honors thesis, a master's level research project, or during doctoral studies. Established researchers working in other paradigms can also learn some of the key principles and practices through extended workshops, which are offered by many research institutes worldwide. Individuals also seek guidance and support for conducting qualitative research through formal and informal mentoring with experienced qualitative researchers; every member of a research team using a mixed-methods approach, for example, can benefit from the expertise in the group, particularly for research practices with which they are not familiar. Wherever a qualitative researcher gets his or her start, there is a long apprentice-style approach involved in learning how to conduct this type of research. Scholars are continually learning new interviewing techniques, ideas about handling ethics challenges, and ways to use technological tools in their research. Here are some of the key areas where education, training, and mentorship are needed:

- Grant-writing techniques
- Research ethics principles and practices
- Research design techniques, including creating research problems, budgeting, etc.
- Data collection and analysis practices
- Appropriate use of technology in data collection, analysis, and writing
- Setting realistic timelines for research projects
- Supervising and delegating tasks to research assistants
- Working on collaborative teams, with community partners, quantitative researchers, etc.
- Writing and dissemination practices

More questions? See #59, #60, and #63.

What Kind of Time Investment Is Needed for a Qualitative Research Study?

Qualitative projects can take a long time to plan and implement. Projects that involve research collaborators, including industry or community partners, may require numerous meetings to identify researchable problems and put a project plan in place. The ethics review process, data collection, analysis, and writing may take several months, or longer, depending on the size and scale of the project. A researcher's first qualitative project will take a lot of time to design and implement, whether that person is a student who is new to research or a senior scholar who is coming to qualitative research for the first time. There are no standards about the length of time a project may take, especially as completion times will also depend on the researcher's other commitments. However, the following list may provide some general guidelines on the key time-related elements that researchers must consider:

- **Project planning and design (4+ months).** Planning a qualitative project can take several months, depending on the size of the project. A doctoral student may spend a full year developing a research proposal, particularly learning about research ethics, new methods for data collection, and other issues while gaining content expertise. A senior researcher with extensive research collaborations may hold several project planning meetings to identify project goals and address the needs of industry and community partners. Conducting background research for specific elements of the project plan (from identifying research sites to pricing data collection equipment) can take several weeks, depending on the number of co-researchers, methods, and locations to be involved in the project.
- **Ethics review (2+ months).** The process of applying for formal ethics review can take several weeks. Although some details can be copied from the project proposal, there are other details in formal ethics applications that are written at this stage. Details on consent

procedures, sample data collection instruments, and other information must be provided at the time of application. Often, research
ethics boards may only meet on a monthly basis; if revisions are
required, a project may be reviewed at subsequent meetings before
final approval is received.

- **Data collection (4+ months).** Data collection can take several
  weeks or months, depending on the number of methods, number
  of research sites, types of data to be gathered, and other details.
  Many qualitative methods also require intense periods of focus on
  the part of the researcher, which can slow the process of data collection. For example, a researcher may find that he or she can only
  conduct a few in-depth interviews in one week, as conducting
  emergent exploratory interviews (i.e., where the questions evolve as
  the interview progresses) requires very focused attention. Data
  preparation and management tasks, including creating backup interview files and transcribing interviews, are also time-consuming. One
  60-minute interview may take a professional transcriptionist up to 4
  hours (and a novice up to 8 hours) to transcribe, depending on the
  quality of the recording, clarity of the speaker's voice, and so on.
- **Analysis (4+ months).** Data analysis typically begins alongside
  data collection in qualitative studies, rather than existing as a discrete and separate stage. That said, there is a period of intensive
  analysis that occurs once all data are gathered. This process can
  take several weeks, months, or even years, depending on the nature
  of the project and methods involved.
- **Dissemination (4+ months).** The writing process in qualitative
  research is also lengthy and may last for several months or years. The
  rich data gathered in these projects can be analyzed from various
  perspectives and using a number of theoretical frameworks, resulting
  in several unique and in-depth reports of results. Where the writing
  process involves engagement with community-based partners, for
  example, dissemination timelines may be longer than in projects that
  focus exclusively on academic publications. The format of dissemination strategies may also range from scholarly conferences, journals
  and books, to professional workshops, seminars and technical
  reports. The writing process involves the integration of extensive
  quotes, typically drawn from transcribed datasets or other textual
  sources, which can take time to collate and present, appropriately,
  for the target audience of the findings.

More questions? See #11, #13, and #89.

Qualitative Research Seems to Be More Expensive to Do Than Other Types of Research—Is That So?

Given the amount of time involved in conducting qualitative research, these projects may seem costly to complete. Fieldwork may require several research assistants to be on the ground for extended periods of time. Because of the emergent nature of the work (e.g., where the types of observational data gathered may be chosen on-site rather than predetermined), research assistants are often hired at the project-planning phase and employed throughout the project. In these cases, personnel costs can be quite substantial. Although all projects may involve travel costs, especially in large-scale national or international projects, the lengthy and in-depth nature of qualitative research can extend the number of project days spent in other cities. This can extend the budgets for these projects, to cover accommodation, meals, and incidental costs over the data collection period. Further, professional transcriptionists, translators, computer programmers, or other expert, technical staff may need to be hired to prepare materials for data collection and analysis.

Despite these costs, many other research approaches are far more expensive than qualitative projects. Typically, qualitative researchers do not require expensive lab equipment, high-powered computing devices, or large teams of personnel to conduct their work. A historian may conduct oral history interviews as a solo scholar, requiring inexpensive equipment (such as a digital recorder), limited travel costs, a single research assistant to provide support, and so on. A sociologist engaging in qualitative content analysis may download documents from an existing computer and not require any staffing, equipment, or other financial supports to complete the project. Compared to large-team biomedical research, for example, which requires substantial personnel and infrastructure costs, qualitative research projects are inexpensive to conduct. In the end, the costs of all projects are relative to discipline and methodology and will depend on the infrastructure needed and types of outputs expected.

More questions? See #13, #63, and #89.

What Are the Limitations of Qualitative Research?

All research projects have limitations that need to be acknowledged in the design and in writing about the results of the study. These limitations may include geographic, cultural, or temporal limitations, meaning that projects present a picture of the world in a particular time and place, within a specific cultural context. These types of project design limitations are common to all types of research, not just qualitative projects. A study that explores girls' experiences is limited in that it cannot provide evidence of boys' experiences. A study that examines workplace politics in for-profit organizations cannot provide evidence related to not-for-profit organizations. While these examples may seem intuitive (as a project cannot be something it is not designed to be), it is important to understand the boundaries of the work so that the findings are not said to be transferable to "all children" or "all organizations" when data have been gathered only within specific contexts. Over time, a researcher may extend the work to include other populations, providing data that can allow for broader transferability through comparative analysis. Or a researcher may extend the reach of the initial findings by using a quantitative design to explore the issues with a larger dataset to provide complementary statistical data to sit alongside the rich qualitative results.

Qualitative research has a number of built in limitations that set this approach apart from other designs. Qualitative designs explore phenomena in depth, typically using multiple methods, rather than gaining only a broad (but surface) glimpse of activities using a single method. For this reason, projects tend to use smaller sample sizes, in fewer locations, and over longer periods of time than most quantitative studies. Qualitative researchers must consider the population to which the findings will be transferred to determine the limitations of the approach. For example, if a study is designed to transfer across genders, the sampling approach cannot be restricted to only women. If the researcher wants to compare within and across genders, the sample size will need to be large enough to provide both within-gender and across-gender comparisons. However, the depth of the data collection and the number of methods used may require a more focused approach so that a project can stay within budget or meet designated timelines. Although all studies have limitations, qualitative researchers need to understand the nature of the limitations relevant to the paradigm, and make design and logistics-based decisions that will ensure quality data within the boundaries of what is possible to explore in the level of depth required.

More questions? See #34, #43, and #90.

ETHICAL ISSUES IN QUALITATIVE RESEARCH

What Are the Researcher's Ethical Responsibilities in Qualitative Practice?

In studies involving human participants, qualitative researchers' primary ethical focus is a duty of care toward their research participants. The individuals who participate in studies, whether interviewees, focus group members, or community-based co-investigators, are researchers' primary concern when it comes to ethical responsibilities. The process of formal ethics review allows a researcher to consider the various ways that participants contribute to, benefit from, or may be harmed by the qualitative research being planned. Issues of privacy, confidentiality, data ownership, co-authorship, consent, representation of findings, and many other issues must be explored and addressed in the design of the study. For example, considering whether participants' names should be anonymized is an important consideration; in some studies, research participants may wish to be identified (where it would be unethical not to respect their wishes), while in other studies, participants' identities may need to be protected. A key consideration is how best to balance the goals of the study, participants' needs, and ethics guidelines that apply in the particular jurisdiction. Researchers need to ensure that participants understand the risks and benefits if they choose to participate in the study, as well as implementing appropriate designs and data management practices that will respect participants' rights.

Qualitative researchers also have ethical responsibilities in relation to team members and other individuals who are involved in the research. Using sound research practices (such as keeping field notes to track research decisions, sharing data files with team members, and managing budgets appropriately) is paramount. Having discussions about co-authorship expectations (such as author order, the role of research assistants in the writing process, and intellectual property rights) should be done at an early stage of the research process. Hiring, supervisory, and budget practices are all important responsibilities of qualitative researchers, where ethics may play a role in the conduct of the research. The concept of "research ethics" extends far beyond the researcher's interactions with human participants. Rather, "ethical practice" is about acting with integrity at all stages of project design, implementation, and dissemination. Where researchers are unsure about the implications of a particular decision, they need to seek guidance from colleagues, research offices, journal editors, granting agencies and other trusted advisors.

More questions? See #18, #20, and #27.

At What Stage of the Research Do I Need to a Get Formal Ethics Review to Talk to People?

Formal ethics review must be completed prior to recruiting participants for data collection. Although the specific details and processes of ethics review may vary by jurisdiction, it is generally accepted that ethics review must be obtained before a project involving human participants begins. At times, researchers may find it difficult to determine when a project "starts," given that initial work for project planning may involve speaking with people about the research design. In these cases, ethics review may not be needed—unless the individual is actually serving as a participant. For example:

- **Supervisors and/or colleagues.** Researchers typically consult with colleagues, mentors, thesis supervisors, and peers when designing and planning a project. These individuals can provide advice about all phases of project design and implementation, as well as dissemination strategies. If these individuals are not research participants in the project, you will not require ethics review to talk to them to seek this type of advice. However, if the study explored how researchers make decisions about project designs, these individuals might *become* participants at some stage in the project. In this case, an ethics review board can provide advice about the best time to seek ethics approval.
- **Librarians and other research support staff.** Librarians, archivists, statisticians, research office staff, and other support staff can provide valuable information to shape the design of a study. Ethics review is not required to consult with these individuals in their professional roles. However, if the study explored how research support staff view their roles in helping academics to conduct research, they might *become* participants in the project. In this case, an ethics review board can provide advice about the best time to seek ethics approval.

- **Community and industry partners.** Researchers may engage with research partners at various stages of the project, from submitting funding requests to disseminating results. In some cases, these individuals will play a vital role in recruiting participants, providing space for data collection, or providing access to a community for research engagement. The partners may be arms-length gatekeepers, who are not participating in the research; or they may be co-investigators, who are fully involved in the design and implementation. The relationship with the researcher will be paramount in making the decision as to when ethics review is necessary, particularly when relationships are long-standing and where partners are involved as participants. The ethics review board can provide advice on when to seek ethics review in these situations.

Researchers need to think carefully about the roles of the people they connect with in designing their studies. If in doubt, researchers should consult with the ethics review board for guidance on the necessity and timing of formal ethics review. Researchers can also start by asking the following questions to determine the scope of a person's role: **Is the person a research participant *in* the study?** If so, ethics review is required prior to recruiting and data collection. **Is the person only acting as a source of information *for* the study?** If they are serving as gatekeepers, providing professional advice, and so on, but not taking the role of a participant, ethics review is not required to seek advice and information.

More questions? See #11, #16, and #22.

What Kinds of Ethics Challenges Do Qualitative Researchers Face, Typically?

Qualitative researchers explore participants' experiences in great depth and on topics that may be very personal, due to the focus on individuals' perceptions of the study topic. At times, participants serve as co-researchers in the investigation, where the relationships among the team members are very close and may extend over several weeks, months, or years. The ethics challenges that arise in many qualitative projects may focus on

- **Researcher-participant relationships.** Qualitative researchers have complex and varied relationships with their participants. Individuals may be recruited for a single session only and not contacted again, or there may be several follow-up meetings over a long period of time. In these studies, researchers may be quite distanced from the participants and only engage during formal data collection sessions. Participatory, community-based projects may reflect long-standing relationships between researchers and community members; here, researchers may engage with the group in different roles, where the "researcher" role is only one of many ways that they are connected to individuals in the group. Managing the ethical issues and obligations in the various relationships is a key point of consideration when designing and implementing qualitative projects.
- **Informed consent processes.** Researchers must ensure that participants understand the implications of their decision to be involved in a study. That decision must be made in the context of understanding the potential harms and benefits that will arise from the study, along with any potential harm they may face. Participants need to understand how their data will be stored, analyzed, and used, including any details relating to how (or if) they will be identified. Researchers need to consider all implications of the design,

including how the data will be used in future, and be sure that participants are informed of these details as part of the consent process. It is also important to understand that consent is a process and does not end with the signing of a consent form or giving a verbal agreement to participate. Due to the emergent nature of qualitative designs, consent may need to be affirmed at various stages of the project to ensure that participants remain comfortable with their decision to engage in the study.

- **Privacy and confidentiality obligations.** Participants share many details of their lives, in confidence, with qualitative researchers, expecting that their data will be treated with respect and addressing relevant privacy considerations. In some cases, anonymizing the participant can ensure that the results cannot be tracked back to that individual. Where individuals are named, there may be some details that are not analyzed or published as part of the research results. Researchers must be clear with participants as to how their privacy and any confidential details will be treated as part of the consent process. Researchers must also understand any legal or other jurisdictional issues that may conflict with their obligations to participants. For example, if a researcher's professional obligations require them to report certain activities (such as a trained teacher required to report a student who expresses a desire to self-harm), these obligations to report must be explained to participants during the consent process, in advance of the participant disclosing such details.

- **Data storage and management practices.** Researchers must store data, consent forms, and other research materials for designated periods of time (often, five years or more), depending on the jurisdiction where they are conducting the research. Removing identifying details from datasets, for example, may require some materials (such as consent forms) to be stored separately from others (such as anonymized raw data files). Digital and paper formats may require different strategies for storage, particularly where researchers may need to update equipment, change offices, or share files with co-investigators during and after the research is completed. Researchers need to plan how best to store and manage project materials when designing the study, so that they can attend to relevant details in the ethics application, and be able to organize and track materials into the future. Where projects are longitudinal in nature, or where comparative analyses occur many years after data are first gathered, these practices may need to be reviewed and adjusted to ensure that data are treated appropriately.

- **Writing and dissemination practices.** When writing the results of projects, researchers must ensure that they abide by obligations made to participants related to how (or whether) they will be identified. This may involve changing real names to pseudonyms, omitting identifying details in cases where people could be identified easily (such as a specific job title), or changing the names of other people or organizations mentioned during data collection (such as a son's name), where those details would inadvertently identify the participant. Photographs, audio files, and other types of data may also need to be omitted or altered to ensure that participants are not identified, unless the participants have chosen to be identified by their image, voice, or other details captured during data collection. The ways that findings (and participants' voices) are represented in publications and other dissemination venues is another key consideration, particularly with respect to how much control participants will have over how their information appears in the final research documents. The timing of the release of results and the specific venues where data will be disseminated are also key issues that may need to be explored with project participants.

More questions? See #16, #27, and #92.

Ethics Approval Seems to Be More Difficult to Obtain for Qualitative Projects. Is That True?

The most difficult ethics approval processes pertain to studies that are of high risk to participants. Studies involving drug trials or invasive medical procedures, for example, are some of the most challenging to address during ethics review. Qualitative studies exploring topics deemed to put a participant at high risk of potential harm, or conducted with vulnerable participant groups, are also very challenging when it comes to ethics review. Ethics review can be considered "difficult" in these situations, as the review process may take more time or involve other considerations, such as legal issues. For example, a high-risk project may be reviewed by a large, central ethics board, rather than by a single reviewer delegated to consider the file locally. Medical projects may also involve multiple boards (such as a university ethics board, as well as a hospital board), which can extend the timeframe for review. In general, the higher the potential risk to participants, the higher the level of ethics scrutiny demanded of the research plan.

Qualitative projects that are deemed of minimal risk to participants may be no more difficult to review than quantitative studies. However, much depends on the specific project design. An anonymous quantitative questionnaire may be "easy" to review, especially if respondents are not being paid or receiving other incentives to participate, and if the topic is not sensitive. The same can be said of qualitative interviews exploring the same topic. However, if participants will be identified, if incentives are used, if the topic is sensitive, or if other contextual issues affect the ethics of the project, the project will require more scrutiny. As qualitative studies are interactive in nature, delving into participants' views in very personal and up-front ways, projects may be viewed as more "risky" than projects where the researcher is distanced from the individuals who are participating. For this reason, it may seem that ethics approval is more difficult to obtain for qualitative projects. However, if the ethics review board includes members with qualitative research expertise, and if researchers present their study designs in ways that address the ethics implications in detail, the review process need not be more difficult than for other types of designs.

More questions? See #13, #16, and #17.

Can I Name My Participants and Their Organization in Publications About My Study?

The decision whether to name a participant or an organization in a study is an important one that will vary depending on the nature of the project. Many researchers choose to anonymize participants as one strategy to protect these individuals' privacy. Participants may not share key details, or may not want to participate in a study at all, if they know that they will be identified in reports of research. In projects where a participants' well-being, employment status, or physical safety may be compromised due to their participation in a study, researchers need to ensure that participants are not named and cannot be identified by others. In order to achieve this, it may be necessary for the researcher to omit specific details (such as a participant's job title or gender) or assign pseudonyms to an organization or the participant's friends and colleagues to ensure that readers of research reports cannot identify the individual participant.

Where an organization needs to be named (such as when the organization, itself, is the site of study and removing the name will compromise other elements of the dataset), a researcher must take great care to ensure that doing so will not identify individual participants. In a large organization (e.g., a university), with a study of 25 members of a large group (i.e., undergraduates), the use of pseudonyms will typically be sufficient to protect individuals' identities. However, if the study includes an interview with the student council president, the researcher may not include the person's role in order to protect his or her identity; in this case, a researcher may assign a pseudonym and describe the person as "involved in campus politics" or "engaged with student-run committees." Balancing the individual's need to be anonymized with content alterations that may affect the study's outcomes is a key point of consideration for all researchers. The end goal is to anonymize or alter only those details that are necessary to protect participants' identities; a blanket approach to anonymity (where the name of the institution, the names of anyone mentioned by participants, etc.) is not appropriate, as the lack of detailed data and transparency about findings can compromise the quality of results.

There are also many cases, however, where participants want to be named in the study. They may want their story to be told, for historical purposes, or they may wish to receive credit for the statements they make. In community-based projects, where the research results are intended to guide changes to practice, it may be inappropriate (and impractical) to anonymize the organization or its staff. In some cultures (such as studies with Indigenous peoples), it may also be an affront to remove the individual's name from the data being shared. In these cases, researchers need to explain the process of naming individuals in the project proposal and ethics application to make clear how consent will be managed in this context. The process can be challenging, for example, when some participants want to be named and others do not. In small organizations or groups, where naming a few people will automatically identify others, it may not be possible to name anyone in order to protect the identities of those wishing to be anonymous.

In the end, the participants' wishes should drive the decision to identify or anonymize individuals in a study. This decision needs to be made in the context of the project's goals and design, with the full and informed consent of participants about the decision, and respecting conflicting views about identification that may arise among participants. Ensuring that participants understand the implications of being named versus being anonymized is a key part of the informed consent process, particularly where the implications of identification may not be immediately known. Researchers need to seek guidance from ethics review boards, colleagues, thesis supervisors, community members, and other trusted advisors in making decisions about how best to manage participant and organization identification.

More questions? See #11, #16, and #27.

I'm Going to Do Focus Groups and I Know I'll Need Ethics Approval for Those—But Can I Examine Postings to Social Media Without Seeking Ethics Approval?

Qualitative projects involving human participants (e.g., in a focus group study) typically require ethics review. It is important to seek guidance from your institution as to when ethics review is needed, since ethics policies and guidelines vary between countries and also depend on the design of your project. However, there are many qualitative research projects that examine the *products* of people's activities, for which ethics review is not needed. When data sources are in the public domain, where they can be accessed by anyone, ethics review is generally not required—even when the individual is named and when other identifying information is available. A good example is when a person writes a letter to the editor of a local newspaper; the published letters typically name the author and may include other identifying details about the person's life. These letters may be a rich source of data for qualitative content analysis and would not require ethics review to study. However, if a person wrote a series of letters that were never sent to the newspaper (and, therefore, never published in the public domain)—and that person offered to give them to the researcher—this *would* require ethics review. In this case, the letters are private documents in the hands of a research participant, which require ethics review to include them in the study.

In some cases, social media postings are similar to letters to the editor—that is, opinion pieces that people post online, in the public domain, to share with other people. These postings may include the author's name and other identifying information, as well as other documents (e.g., family photos). When these postings are in the public domain, ethics review is not required for research use. However, researchers must be very careful to understand the nature of the social media platform used and whether the information they want to access is truly "public" or actually residing in a "private" Internet space. Where information is posted within a private group (e.g., where individuals must formally join a Facebook group to access members' posting), researchers generally treat these as private postings that require ethics review for access. Although some individuals may share information publicly on social media, other individuals ensure that their privacy settings restrict access to postings to a select group of people. Accessing these private postings requires ethics review.

Even when a project does not require a formal ethics review process, researchers must take care to treat all datasets in an ethically responsible way. Formal ethics review addresses specific types of research practices, where human participants are involved (e.g., interviews, questionnaires, focus groups, private diaries). When data are publically available, researchers may still need to make ethical choices about the treatment of those data. For example, if a Web discussion is of a very sensitive nature (e.g., postings related to personal health diagnoses), a researcher may decide not to publish the name of a person posting to a public website, if those identifiers are not germane to the analysis.

More questions? See #16, #52, and #70.

Can I Show My Colleague Some Transcripts and Let Her Listen to Interview Recordings to Get Advice on My Interpretation of the Data?

When designing a research project, it is important to consider who will have access to your data and for what purpose. In some cases, qualitative researchers want to use colleagues and others (such as community stakeholders) to review findings arising from the project to see whether the themes are credible and make sense given the evidence gathered. When using a formal review process, such as intercoder reliability checking, the researcher provides copies of transcripts, codebooks, and other contextual materials so that independent coders can assess the appropriateness of assigned themes and categories. In peer debriefing sessions, researchers may seek advice from colleagues based on excerpts of transcripts or discussions of the themes that are emerging in the analysis. Depending on the nature of the project, recorded data may be shared in raw form (e.g., reviewing a video recording of a focus group to discuss the nature of the group interaction observed).

In all cases, the primary concern of the researcher is focused on the protection of participants involved in the research activity. There are many ethics implications involved in sharing data outside of the research team, which must be addressed in ethics approvals related to the project. For example, if the ethics application for the project notes that data will be anonymized prior to publication of results, it is important that transcripts and excerpts are anonymized prior to sharing these with colleagues. If the ethics application states that audio recordings are only for the use of the researcher, data cannot be shared with others in that form; an amendment may be required to the ethics protocol or a researcher may only be able to share excerpts of the data that do not identify the participants. It may also be necessary to show—rather than give—materials to colleagues to ensure that the researcher is managing and storing the data appropriately, at all times. For example, will sharing data in a cloud storage system (such as DropBox) provide the necessary safeguards for the data? Will showing video recordings in an office space with an open design format mean that others may overhear participants' interviews? Researchers need to consider how they will provide the data to their colleagues, including the privacy, storage, and management implications of those decisions.

More questions? See #16, #17, and #87.

The Ethics Review Board Requires Me to Submit My Interview Questions—But the Project Is Exploratory and the Questions Will Emerge as the Interview Happens. What Types of Questions Should I Submit for Review?

Most ethics review processes require researchers to provide copies of data collection instruments to allow the ethics committee to understand the nature of participants' engagement in the data collection process. In qualitative research, researchers may need to provide copies of interview guides, participant diary templates, vignettes to be shared with participants, and other materials to be used in the project.

As qualitative approaches are emergent in design, it is unlikely that researchers will know all of the questions that will be asked of participants in advance of data collection. New questions will be added to an interview guide as new topics emerge after the initial interviews; other questions may be dropped if they are not relevant to participants' experiences. However, the nature of the project is guided by the research questions being addressed with the chosen methods. Researchers can provide the initial questions they plan to ask, which speak to the boundaries of the project, so that the ethics committee can see the scope of the topics to be addressed. Using a phrase such as "Questions may include, but are not limited to, the following:" may be useful in outlining the design of questions in the ethics application. Including possible prompts in the guide (such as "if the answer is no, I will then ask questions about the reasons for this answer") will also demonstrate the emergent nature of the process, while satisfying the committee's need to see the nature of the questions to be asked. Similarly, if a researcher plans to ask interviewees to share examples of policy documents for discussion, a sample document could be appended to the ethics application to show the type of material that may be discussed. It is important to balance the committee's need to get a feel for the data collection process, while respecting the emergent, exploratory nature of qualitative research designs.

More questions? See #16, #30, and #31.

The Ethics Review Board Says I Have to Destroy My Data, but I Think My Analysis Will Take Years. Do I Have to Destroy Everything?

The decision to destroy data—or to store data, permanently—will vary, project by project. This is an important decision and one that is made by the research team, not the ethics review board. Typically, ethics review boards will expect researchers to outline how they plan to follow data retention guidelines in place in their institutions. For example, a university may require research data to be stored for a minimum period of time (such as five years) to satisfy government regulations. Researchers must store all data files, consent materials, project management files, and other documents related to the research for these minimum periods. If they decide to destroy their data, researchers will outline those plans in the ethics application, including in information letters to be shared with study participants.

It is important to note that minimum retention guidelines do not require data destruction at the end of that period. The choice to destroy the dataset resides with the research team and depends on various factors. Longitudinal studies, for example, may require data to be stored long-term to allow for comparative analyses. Similarly, studies that gather data of national or international significance that involve sensitive health or financial data, or that document ongoing processes of product development, may need to be stored for many years. In some cases, researchers may wish to deposit the dataset in an archive for later use by other scholars or community members. All of these choices must be made at the design phase of the project and outlined in the ethics materials so that participants are informed about the intentions for data storage and plans (if any) for destruction.

Researchers need to reflect on the short- and long-term goals of their projects and make informed decisions about data storage and retention at the time they complete their ethics applications. Relevant institutional and/or government regulations must be consulted as part of this process so the research team can develop an appropriate approach to data storage that best suits the needs of the study and the participants.

More questions? See #16, #73, and #96.

I Have Learned Negative Things About People in the Setting I'm Studying. How Do I Deal With This?

Qualitative researchers learn a great deal about people when conducting their research, whether these details are about the participants themselves or about other people with whom the participant engages. The degrees of positivity and negativity can vary tremendously and depend on the researcher's perspective on the issue. As qualitative researchers design their studies in neutral ways so that they do not impose their biases, worldviews, and perspectives on participants, deciding whether to view an incident as "positive" or "negative" may well depend on the participants' views. Participants in a study of workplace bullying, for example, may see this phenomenon as something very toxic, which is adversely affecting work practices and, therefore, needs to be eliminated. Or participants may see workplace bullying as having positive outcomes, presenting opportunities for personal growth, resilience, and the development of new skills in managing conflicts with others. Typically, seeing the issue through the participants' eyes and interpreting the results of the study, without passing judgment on participants' motives and actions, will ensure that negative and positive results are managed in respectful and appropriate ways.

In some cases, a researcher may learn something that he or she views as negative about the participants. A participant may disclose that he or she has engaged in inappropriate behavior in the workplace. The researcher will need to decide how to write about this disclosure so that the participant's views and the description of events are presented in ways that are true to the data and relevant to the analysis. Where the researcher's personal views may conflict with those of the participant, this decision can be difficult. At times, researchers need to present the analytical narrative in ways that present the participant in a negative light; however, suppressing these data, or choosing to omit elements of the data to present the participant in positive terms, would damage the integrity of the data. Where long-term relationships exist between researchers and participants, particularly when these relationships are integral to ongoing research in the study site, these situations will need to be navigated carefully.

More questions? See #11, #16, and #27.

My Ethics Approval Says That I Have to Let the Board Know if There Are "Significant Changes" to My Methodology and/or Method. As My Qualitative Study Is Exploratory and Emergent in Design, How Do I Know When a Significant Change Has Occurred?

A significant change to a research design is one that alters the intent of the study, the process by which data will be gathered, or both. The emergent nature of the study means that specific questions on an interview guide, or specific points of observation, cannot be known fully before the study begins. During an ethics review process, a researcher provides an interview guide or an observational guide that demonstrates the scope and intent of the data to be gathered. The boundaries of the core areas to be explored are determined by the research questions, so data collection instruments can address those boundaries prior to the start of data collection.

Once in the field, researchers will find that the wording of specific questions, the specific micro-topics discussed, and the number of observational sites may change, depending on what is learned at the early stages of data collection and analysis. For this reason, researchers will build some flexibility into the project proposal (and ethics application) to account for these changes. Providing a range of the number of participants to be recruited (such as 18 to 25), or examples of the prompts that will be asked during an interview (such as "Why did you feel that way?" or "What did you do next?"), will provide a general guideline to external reviewers as to how data collection will proceed.

A significant change, then, includes one where the focus of data collection to address specific research questions needs to be altered. Once in the field, a researcher may realize that there is another group of key stakeholders he or she needs to interview or that the original observational activities exclude an important area to be examined. Changes to the method, methodology, and design of the activities would need to be outlined in an amended ethics application. Similarly, changes to recruiting strategies may constitute a significant change, which is quite common when researchers are not sure of the best ways to connect with potential participants. In these cases, it is best to include a range of strategies in the ethics application (such as posters, direct e-mail, snowball techniques) so that a researcher does not need to go back to the ethics review process with each small change to the protocol. Planning for a "worst case" scenario and planning flexible strategies to account for emergent design will ease the ethics review process in many cases. And getting advice from the ethics board members, colleagues, thesis supervisors, and others as to what will constitute a "significant change" at the time of the original ethics application will ensure that researchers are taking appropriate steps and seeking ethics amendments when appropriate.

More questions? See #18, #31, and #61.

One of My Participants Told Other People That She Was Involved in My Study, Even Though I Promised I Would Not Identify Her. Is This a Problem?

Research participants often share their experiences as study participants with other people, even when the research team has promised not to discuss the participants' involvement in the project. A researcher's responsibility is to uphold promises made as part of the informed consent process. If a participant was guaranteed anonymity, so the researcher promised not to identify that person, the researcher must do everything they can to ensure that the person is not identified. This may involve, for example, assigning a pseudonym to the participant's quotes in publications or not revealing specific job titles or other details, when doing so would identify the participant. In focus groups or other methods where other participants know one another's identities, the researcher may also ask all group members to agree to follow confidentiality guidelines and not identify one another as participants in the study. However, individual participants are free to share their research experiences with others. Even in these cases, a researcher must ensure that they abide by the promises made to the participant. If they are asked to confirm whether an individual participated, for example, or if they are asked to comment on a participant's statements about what they said during an interview, the researcher cannot disclose this information to others. This can put the researcher in an uncomfortable position, particularly if a participant self-discloses at a public event (such as a conference session where the researcher is sharing—anonymous—results of the study). However, the researcher's obligations to the participants do not change, even if the participants decide to tell others about their involvement.

More questions? See #16, #18, and #92.

PART 3

DESIGNING QUALITATIVE RESEARCH

What Is a Qualitative Research Problem—And How Does This Inform the Development of Research Questions?

The research problem statement describes the point of focus for the project, including the rationale and need for the study itself. Research problems arise from many places:

- The existing research literature, where knowledge gaps or limitations are noted
- Practice environments, where research is needed to examine or explain a phenomenon
- The researcher's prior studies, where new areas for future investigation were noted
- Collaborative research needs, where community, industry, or fellow researchers shape the direction of the research

These influences do not sit in isolation; rather, a researcher links these four elements together (as appropriate), so that the existing literature serves to justify the need for the study, alongside any practice-related or collaborative research needs. All of these must be framed within the context of the researcher's current and prior work so that the project is a clear fit for his or her areas of expertise.

The first step in the process is to develop an overarching research problem statement, which articulates the need for the project, as well as its scope. A researcher may use the following prompting statements in developing the problem:

"The goal of this study is to…"

"To date, research has examined [X]; however, very few studies explore [Y]…"

"By using a qualitative design with [Z] as a methodological framework…"

"This study is significant for practice, because…"

"The project will contribute to scholarly knowledge by…"

Once the overarching problem statement has been crafted, qualitative researchers then identify a few (typically, five or six) core research questions that will be explored in the study. Often, there will be a separate set of questions for each methodology or method to be used in the study so that the researcher can set out the boundaries of the investigation for each approach. For example, research questions that shape a study of nurses' experiences may be structured as follows:

"What does it mean to work as a nurse in a hospital setting?"

"What are the benefits and/or limitations to working as part of a health care team?"

"How do nurses view themselves in relation to physicians, pharmacists, and other health care practitioners?"

The key thing to keep in mind is that these are questions aimed at the researcher, which guide the development of the study. Specific interview or focus group questions, aimed at nurses, for example, will be developed later, once the project design is complete.

More questions? See #1, #30, and #31.

What Is the Role of a Hypothesis in Qualitative Research?

A hypothesis does not have a central role in qualitative research. Hypotheses are used in deductive, quantitative projects; a statement is made at the beginning of the project and then that theory is tested in data collection and analysis. Qualitative projects explore data related to research questions, which are typically informed by an overarching research problem statement. The research project is inductive, with theory generated from data.

A quantitative researcher may generate a hypothesis based on the results of a qualitative study, which is then tested using a quantitative design. Or, a hypothesis used in a quantitative project may raise interesting research questions for qualitative researchers, who then design qualitative projects to explore the issues in more depth. In mixed-methods projects, the design will have both hypotheses and research questions, with each informing the design of the quantitative and qualitative components of the study, respectively.

More questions? See #6, #8, and #55.

What Is an Exploratory Qualitative Design? If I Do This, Does It Mean That My Research Isn't Going to Come Up With "Usable" Findings?

Qualitative research projects are described as exploratory when they examine an issue for the first time, in-depth, within a given setting, context, or with particular types of participants. Existing research into the phenomenon of interest, for example, may focus exclusively on quantitative results that provide broad, surface results about a particular issue. Here, the unique contribution of a qualitative study is to explore, for the first time, the meaning of the topic from participants' own perspectives, to complement and extend the quantitative results. In other cases, the topic may be very new, with few published results in any discipline or using any research paradigm. A qualitative design can examine the nature of the topic, when little at all is known about the nature of the phenomenon.

The question of whether exploratory data are "usable" relates to the quality of the data gathered. Although some researchers may (mistakenly!) believe that exploratory qualitative studies are only useful as a means to get some ideas to design robust quantitative studies, exploratory results can be trustworthy and transferable in their own right. When data are gathered appropriately, using established standards for the implementation of the method, the results will be sound; if the sample size is large enough for saturation, the data will also be transferable beyond the sample under study.

That is not to say that exploratory results cannot or should not be used to create other, future project designs. This is a useful and pragmatic approach to research design, where initial, exploratory work informs the design of other methods or explorations in other settings and situations. Just as quantitative results can identify areas where in-depth qualitative data would provide useful insights, so too can qualitative results point to areas where surface-level, quantitative data drawn from large samples can provide useful contextual results.

More questions? See #31, #55, and #90.

What Is an Emergent Qualitative Design?

The word *emergent* is often used to describe qualitative research because of the inductive nature of the design. An emergent design is one that evolves and changes during project implementation. A researcher begins a project by designing a particular methodological approach, using specific methods for data collection, based on existing evidence related to the population, setting, and context under investigation. As qualitative projects are primarily inductive and exploratory, the final design emerges as data collection and analysis progress. In this way, a researcher can be responsive to the realities of the context, adjusting the research design to suit the specific situation, at the moment of data collection. Rather than imposing a design that may not be an appropriate fit for the participants, sites, or texts chosen for analysis (and then changing the study design in future weeks, months, or years later), an emergent design allows for built-in flexibility so that the study design is attuned to the needs of the research context.

For example, consider a research project that uses a case study methodology to explore the use of social media by for-profit organizations. The researcher decides to use interviews with managers, focus groups with staff, and document analysis of information technology policies to gather relevant data. Once on-site, during data collection, the researcher learns there are other policy documents related to staffing profiles that also need to be examined. Or, the researcher learns staff are holding back information during the focus groups because of fears that sharing perspectives in front of colleagues will be damaging to their careers. The researcher may decide to add individual interviews to the process and to include a broader range of policy documents in the analysis to obtain a more complete picture of the research topics under study. In this way, an emergent design acknowledges that researchers will not have all the knowledge they need, in hand, before they enter the field. Although changes to the design may require ethics review amendments (in cases where a change in design has not been fully outlined in the original application), these changes will result in datasets that are more responsive and relevant to the research questions outlined in the project proposal.

More questions? See #1, #6, and #30.

What Is the Role of a Theoretical and/or Conceptual Framework in a Qualitative Study?

A conceptual framework is an overarching set of beliefs, theories, and perspectives that shape the design of the research project. Often these are determined by the existing research literature, where a new study is designed to build on prior knowledge about a phenomenon. However, the conceptual framework is also informed by the specific methodology chosen for the project. A project that uses a grounded theory approach, for example, will look very different from a phenomenology, or a narrative inquiry, or a discourse analysis project. The researcher's worldview and epistemological stance also shape the research and contribute to the conceptual framework applied in a given study.

The role of theory in qualitative research will vary with the project design. As qualitative research is inductive, theory is not identified and "tested" in the project design. However, existing theories about how people engage with the world around them may well inform the project's goals, ethical design, the methodology and methods selected, and the ways that the researcher engages with the participants. A feminist conceptual framework, for example, will be informed by various feminist theories (such as standpoint theory); a qualitative design will position feminist principles at the heart of the research design, which will affect the research problem statement, research questions, methodology, method, data analysis, and writing practices. In other designs, the application of existing theories may come much later, once data are gathered and begin to shape the interpretations made by the researcher. In these cases, theory may be used to help the researcher to understand what they are seeing in the field. Further, the project design may be focused on theory generation, rather than application; in these cases, theories of human behavior are developed at the analysis stage as the data unfold.

More questions? See #5, #33, and #78.

How Extensive Should My Literature Review Be When I'm Designing My Project?

Researchers need to consider a range of literature when designing their projects. Existing research published in the discipline will need to be reviewed, as well as literature from related disciplines. A project exploring young children's use of toys to enhance online reading activities, for example, may draw on literature in education, information science, psychology, computing science, and other relevant areas. Although the emphasis may be on the most current literature so that the project builds on previous work in a timely way, key historic works must also be addressed so that the new work is well grounded in the core literature of the discipline.

In addition to literature relevant to the topic of the research, researchers also need to consult a range of methods texts and published research when selecting the methodology and method(s) to be used in the project. Being able to ground the project in the "best practices" of research design is key to project success, but also useful when a proposal is being made to granting agency, supervisory committee, community-based organization, or another peer-review process. Although positioning the research in the content area is key to justify the need for the work, researchers must also ground the project in the established methods literature relevant to the design. Being able to justify project design decisions, and to highlight any innovative methodological details, will ensure a strong project proposal.

Researchers also need to remember that a literature review is an ongoing process, rather than something that ends at the point of project design. Keeping up with current literature to ensure that the research is responsive to newly published work is vital. However, as qualitative research is inductive, emergent, and focused on theory building, the literature will also guide the development of the project as it unfolds. New topic areas may be identified or existing theoretical frameworks may inform data analysis, so researchers are continually reading and considering the literature as the data are gathered.

More questions? See #2, #12, and #32.

What Kinds of Sampling Approaches Are Appropriate for Qualitative Studies?

Qualitative projects are typically designed using nonprobabilistic sampling methods. Unlike quantitative studies (where the goal is to generalize to a larger population, therefore requiring a formal representative sample for statistical purposes), qualitative projects use sampling approaches designed to recruit people and texts that will allow for theoretical and conceptual explanations of the topic being studied. This approach requires a purposive, selective approach to sampling that fits with the inductive (theory-building) intentions of qualitative research. Qualitative researchers will often start with a unique, particular site or group of individuals or documents, and then look for similar or different cases based on the concepts that emerge in the early stages of data collection. There are a number of sampling approaches used in qualitative studies to achieve this goal; this list outlines some of the most common approaches:

- **Purposive (or Theoretical) Sampling.** In this approach, people, sites, and documents are chosen because they meet specific inclusion criteria for the study. An individual may fit a particular demographic profile (e.g., teenage boys), have a specific job title (e.g., CEOs of information technology companies), or have experienced a particular phenomenon (e.g., a resident of New Orleans who survived Hurricane Katrina). A text may be published by a particular entity (e.g., the federal government), be aimed at a particular audience (e.g., high school textbooks), or reflect a particular topic (e.g., guides for parents on managing children's asthma). As data collection moves ahead, the researcher may also sample across a range of experiences within the set inclusion criteria; for example, if a study of teenage boys begins by recruiting only 13- and 14-year-olds, the researcher may focus on recruiting older teens in the later phases of the project to provide a range of experiences and perspectives.

- **Maximum Variation Sampling.** This is a specific form of purposive sampling where the researcher sets out to recruit individuals, sites, or texts that reflect diversity to be able to theorize across groups. A study of library users might include people of various ages, a mix of genders, different employment status, or various cultural backgrounds. Or, the approach may be used to sample for divergent experiences of the topic under study; a study of seniors' comfort with technology might include people who are very comfortable, as well as those who are very uncomfortable, and everything in between. The focus of analysis in this type of sampling approach is on commonalities across the diverse group of participants or texts recruited to the study.
- **Snowball Sampling.** In some cases, especially where recruiting individuals may be difficult, researchers rely on the initial participants or texts to lead to new potential recruits. A study of people grieving the loss of a spouse may ask initial participants to pass the study's details on to other people in their social circle to recruit new participants. A content analysis study may rely on the cited references or other details in the initial document set to identify additional materials for review. In some cases, snowball sampling is used to identify new participants that are *not* like the initial participant group. For example, if a person grieving the loss of a spouse is coping very well, the researcher may ask them to pass the study details to someone who is struggling; this allows for a breadth of experience in the participant group.

More questions? See #15, #35, and #43.

Why Are Sample Sizes So Small in Many Qualitative Studies? Isn't This a Problem?

Qualitative studies are often criticized for their small sample sizes; however, this criticism points to a general lack of understanding about the nature of qualitative research. Different sample sizes (and types) are needed depending on the intention of the project design. Large sample sizes are often required in quantitative projects, for example, where the goal of the study is to analyze results for statistical significance and to be able to make claims about (and to generalize to) the broader population. The data collection techniques used in these studies (such as questionnaires) are designed to provide a broad, surface glimpse of a phenomenon; large samples of people can be studied, at low cost, providing robust datasets for statistical analysis and generalization. As the goal of qualitative research is to dig into an issue, in-depth, and provide rich data that examine what it is like for people experiencing a phenomenon, smaller sample sizes are appropriate and will vary with the specific methods being employed. The goal of the project is to be able to transfer findings across groups, with subsequent studies designed to extend those findings across different geographic regions, populations, cultural contexts, and so on.

The depth of data collection and analysis in qualitative research is such that smaller sample sizes at the individual case level are appropriate, both in terms of the time and costs needed to gather data, as well as the amount of data available for analysis. As most qualitative projects involve some form of triangulation, referring to the number of participants, alone, to give a sense of the scale of the study can be misleading. A project involving interviews with 20 people, for example, may follow those individuals for several months. A researcher may conduct multiple interviews with each person, resulting in hundreds of hours of recordings and thousands of pages of transcripts. These individuals may also be asked to keep diaries of their experiences, to draw maps of their social networks, or to provide photographs from their childhood. Subsequent interviews may be conducted with family members, colleagues, or employers to get a clear sense of the issues being explored from a range of perspectives. The scale and depth of the various data collection methods should be clearly articulated in grant proposals, journal articles, and conference presentations so that readers get a clear sense of the scope of what will be analyzed.

More questions? See #34, #39, and #43.

What Is the Ideal Sample Size for a Qualitative Project?

Deciding on the number of research sites and individual cases to include in a qualitative study is a difficult decision. Much will depend on the context of the study, the norms of the discipline, the logistics involved in data collection, and other factors. In some cases, relatively small sample sizes are appropriate and desirable; in others, large-scale qualitative designs will be the best choice for the research questions. Although there is no "ideal" sample size, there are a number of questions researchers can ask to help them in making this decision:

1. **What are the norms in my research discipline?** In some disciplines, a sample of one is sufficient to gather quality data and publish quality work. Autoethnography and case-study methodologies, for example, may involve a single person or site as the focal point for the research. Even in these approaches, however, data are often gathered over long periods and using multiple data sources, which results in a rich dataset for analysis. In other disciplines, there may be an expectation of a much larger sample, which is believed to provide more robust data to inform the transferability of results. A researcher aiming for saturation of themes, for example, may aim for 15 to 25 individual participants, where saturation typically occurs. A researcher working in a discipline that is heavily quantitative in nature (and where a minimum "n" of 30 is the norm) may involve many more participants or sites in their studies. It is important to keep in mind that it is not just the individual or the site that matters here, but the number of methods, the depth of the approach, and the amount of data that will be generated; at times, fewer sites or people may need to be involved because of the types of data that will be generated. All of these elements contribute to the "size" of the sample, not just the raw number of participants.

2. **Do I want to be able to compare across groups or identify common patterns only?** Many researchers are interested in comparisons, across gender lines, age, or other demographics, or from

site to site. If a researcher wants to present comparative data in the analysis, the sample size will need to be greater than if he or she were presenting findings drawn from across the whole group. For example, a researcher sampling to saturation of common themes across a maximum variation sample of interviews may aim for 15 to 25 participants, total. However, if the researcher wants to present data on men's versus women's perceptions of the research phenomenon, the sample would need to be 15 to 25 men *and* 15 to 25 women—or a total of 30 to 50 participants. Similarly, if the intention of the study was to present data across genders (without comparison), but only 1 male participant volunteered out of 25 participants, the researcher could not claim that the findings were transferable to all. The researcher would need to recruit more men, purposively, to present a balance of perspectives, or reframe the study to focus on females' perspectives alone.

3. **How much money, time, equipment, and so on, do I have to complete the research?** Logistics and infrastructure are important factors to consider when deciding on sample size. Some researchers cannot afford to travel or may need to complete the data collection within a restricted timeframe. For these reasons, the sample size may be less than ideal because of factors beyond the researcher's control. In these cases, a researcher may decide to treat the initial work as a pilot phase, gathering more data in the future, once additional resources are available. In other cases, a researcher may choose to complement a small sample in one method (such as a small number of key informant interviews) with more data in another method, which is more logistically feasible in the situation (such as a discourse analysis of policy documents, where there are no travel costs or other expenses). In the end, the quality of the dataset is paramount; a small sample size may be a problem—or it may not—depending on the research goals of the project.

More questions? See #13, #39, and #43.

How Do You Recruit Participants for a Qualitative Study?

R ecruiting participants for a study is a key concern for qualitative researchers, particularly where the types of people to be involved may be difficult to reach. As the time investment for participants can vary tremendously, depending on the design (from a 30-minute interview to a series of multi-hour sessions), researchers also need to consider whether incentives are appropriate. Where a participant will be asked to devote a great deal of time to a project, financial or other forms of compensation may be warranted. Ethics issues must also be considered in recruiting so that participants are not coerced, but feel free to say "no" to the researcher, without any personal consequences. Where the researcher is a participant of a group or in a position of power, for example, recruiting activities must be carefully managed to ensure that participants feel free to opt out of the project.

Researchers use a number of different approaches to recruit potential participants, including

- **Posters, brochures, mailed flyers, newspaper ads, and other approaches using visual designs.** Hospital waiting rooms, shopping malls, libraries, and other locations that receive a lot of public traffic are ideal places to post recruiting notices on bulletin boards or to leave brochures about a study. Some researchers will also put notices in community newspapers or organizational newsletters to solicit recruits. Permission needs to be obtained to do so, and fees may be required, but getting an ad in front of members of the public can be an effective way to recruit individuals to participate.
- **E-mail and other distribution lists.** Sending notices to potential recruits directly (e.g., to e-mail lists that are publicly available on websites) can be an effective way of getting participants. However, sending to group lists (such as an open call on a Listserv, where potential participants are registered) is also a useful strategy. In some cases, permissions may be needed or the notice may need to be circulated by a third party.

- **Seeking volunteers when conducting other methods.** In mixed- or multi-method studies, using an initial method (such as a questionnaire or a focus group) to solicit participants for the next phase of research (such as a one-on-one interview) can be a good strategy for recruitment.
- **Other people.** Once a few individuals or organizations have been recruited, researchers can also use these connections to solicit other participants through a technique known as snowball sampling. Similarly, researchers may rely on their co-investigators, colleagues, students, community partners, industry contacts, and others to spread the word about the study.
- **Social media.** Researchers are using social media increasingly to recruit participants to their studies. If the population under study is active on Facebook, Twitter, or other media, posting study details and a link to a project website can be an effective way to communicate with potential participants. The design of these tools also allows people to share the notices with their own networks so that a large number of potential participants can be contacted.

More questions? See #11, #36, and #74.

I Really Want to Use Focus Groups, So How Can I Design a Project That Will Use That Method?

Qualitative research projects are designed to address the research questions identified by the researcher(s) involved. The choice of a particular method must be made only after the research questions have been outlined, as the methodology and method(s) needed to address those questions must fit with the project's overall goals. For this reason, starting a new project by saying, "I want to use focus groups," or "I want to design a mixed-methods study" is not the right approach to take for appropriate, sound research design. Depending on the nature of the research problem being investigated, a focus group (or other method) may or may not be the best choice to get at the types of data needed. A researcher that begins by driving a study toward the use of a particular method will find the creative work of project design is severely restricted at a very early stage in project development. For example, a focus group may not be appropriate to use with particular methodologies; if the methodology is designed to explore individuals' life histories or personal narratives, a group approach may not produce the type (or depth) of data needed for analysis.

Even where the focus group is a good fit for a specific methodology, the nature of the method (such as the influence of strong personalities in shaping the discussion) may not be the best choice with particular study topics, populations, or settings. Although focus groups may be excellent choices for market research, where individuals are shown an advertisement and asked to comment, studies that require longitudinal data, or individual use of a computer interface, may be best suited to individual interviews. Thinking about any method, first, constrains the location of data collection, the timeline for completion, who gathers and analyzes the data, the types of data collection equipment needed, and other specific plans for the study. This happens in quantitative projects as well, where researchers start by saying, "I want to use SurveyMonkey to design a questionnaire," even where that method (and/or the online tool for gathering data) is not the best choice for the project's goals. If logistics, infrastructure, and other elements of the project design cannot fit with a focus group (or other method), a researcher will struggle to fit that method into the project plan and, in the end, may not gather the data that are needed.

Researchers ask the following questions in determining the method best suited to the project:

1. What is the goal of the project? What research questions will the project address?

2. What is my (and my co-researchers') epistemology or epistemological worldview? What methodology is the best fit given this worldview?

3. What method(s) might be a good choice to address the research questions, in the context of the methodology chosen for the study?

   a. Is a mixed-methods design needed for the research problem being investigated? If so, how will the qualitative and quantitative methods complement each other?

   b. Is a multi-methods qualitative approach needed for triangulation? If so, what methods will work best together to meet the project's goals?

   c. Who on the research team has expertise in the relevant method(s) to support the implementation of the design?

4. What logistics and/or infrastructure constraints exist in the design (e.g., available time, money, equipment, travel, etc.) and how will these affect the method choice?

More questions? See #5, #28, and #46.

What Is Triangulation?

Triangulation allows a researcher to investigate the research problem from a variety of angles and perspectives. This approach can help to ensure that the data gathered in a project are credible (i.e., aiding the rigorous design and implementation of the project), but is also very useful in extending the scope of data gathering and analysis, particularly in projects that are exploratory or designed to be emergent. In these cases, the focus of the project—and, therefore, the need for new data—may evolve as the data collection and analysis progress. Gathering data using a triangulated approach provides a more fulsome picture of the phenomenon under study than what would be possible if data were gathered from only one source. At times, triangulation may highlight discrepancies or gaps in a dataset that require further study. For example, when we *ask* people what they do (e.g., what websites do you use?), they may give an answer that is incomplete—not because they want to deceive, but because they cannot remember all the details. By installing a screen-capture program on their computer, the researcher can gather information *in the moment* to see if there are other details that need to be discussed with the participant or addressed in the analysis.

Triangulation may involve the use of multiple methods, different sites, a variety of participant types, or a mix of other variables deemed relevant to the project. A researcher may also design a mixed-methods study, where triangulation occurs across both qualitative (e.g., interviews) and quantitative (e.g., questionnaires) data elements in the research design. In the following example, the researcher would explore the various settings, people, and activities in which young children engage to explore the implications of technology on the learning process. Here, triangulation occurs at multiple levels—i.e., of the methods, sites, and participant groups. As the project evolves, the researcher may realize that additional elements of triangulation are needed (e.g., to include other participant groups or new documents for analysis) to provide sufficient, relevant data for analysis to proceed.

Research Problem:

How do young children engage with technology as part of early literacy learning?

Table 39.1. Modes of Triangulation

Triangulation of Methods	Triangulation of Sites	Triangulation of Sources	Triangulation of Participants
Interviews	Preschool	Transcripts	Teachers, children
Interviews	Child's home	Transcripts	Parents, children
Observation	Preschool classroom	Video-recordings	Teachers, children
Observation	Child's home	Video-recordings	Parents, children
Text analysis	Preschool & school board	Policy documents, teaching materials	Teachers, administrators
Text analysis	Home & public library	Parent handbooks, library resources for children	Parents, children, teachers

More questions? See #9, #35, and #41.

PART 4

ENSURING RIGOR IN QUALITATIVE RESEARCH DESIGN

I've Heard That Quantitative Research Is More Rigorous Than Qualitative Research—Is That True?

Quantitative research is not *more* rigorous than qualitative research; it is *differently* rigorous. In quantitative research, assessment of the validity (i.e., measures what it intends to measure) and reliability (i.e., can be repeated in the future or by others, with the same results) speaks to the rigor of the work. Sampling procedures, data collection tools, and other elements of study design will affect the validity and reliability of a project, so these various elements undergo a great deal of scrutiny in assessing the value of the project. In quantitative research, the rigor of the work will affect the ability of the study to generalize to the broader population, which is an important goal of the project design.

In qualitative projects, rigorous projects are those that are deemed *trustworthy*. Although some qualitative researchers will describe their studies as "valid" and "reliable," other researchers use different terms to describe the rigorous nature of their projects. In this way, researchers have established their own language of rigor, as distinguished from rigor in quantitative designs, which cannot be used to evaluate qualitative research. Over the last few decades, there are many terms that have been used to describe elements of rigor in qualitative studies. These terms include, but are not limited to, the following:

- **Credible, Accurate, or Authentic.** The ability to present the participants' multiple realities in the findings of the research so that they "ring true" to people holding similar beliefs.
- **Confirmable, Authoritative, or Neutral.** Ensuring that the findings are the product of the participants' data, not the perspectives of the researcher.
- **Transferable or Applicable.** The degree to which the findings can be applied to other contexts and settings.
- **Dependable or Consistent.** The degree to which the findings would be repeated if conducted with the same participants or in

similar settings. Although variability is expected in qualitative research, the variability can be tracked and explained. Anomalous data are embraced and included in the findings.

More questions? See #8, #41, and #43.

What Are Effective Strategies for Promoting Trustworthiness?

Designing and implementing a project that can be trusted is an important goal of all research. In order for research to have a positive impact on the world, the users of that research must be assured that the results have emerged through a process that is systematic, rigorous, and trustworthy. Trustworthiness in qualitative research is achieved by designing and implementing projects that are credible, dependable, and confirmable so that the findings may be transferable across populations, settings, or contexts. Trustworthy project designs are those with congruent methodological and methods designs, using triangulation of approaches, where appropriate. Research questions should be neutral in their design, providing boundaries for the study, while maintaining flexibility to support emergent design. Sampling strategies need to provide sufficient, relevant data for saturation of themes in data analysis. Researchers need to develop strategies to manage, track, and review data throughout project implementation to maintain integrity during data collection and analysis. Field notes, data recordings, descriptive codebooks, and other tools allow researchers to document data and analytic decisions. These materials enhance trustworthiness by documenting the systematic processes by which data are gathered, documented, and analyzed.

More questions? See #39, #40, and #64.

I've Heard That Qualitative Studies Suffer From Researcher Bias. How Do I Deal With This Criticism?

Qualitative researchers acknowledge and embrace personal bias in their study designs. Unlike quantitative researchers, who aim to eliminate bias, qualitative researchers believe that bias is always present. A researcher brings a particular worldview to the research questions asked, as well as the design of the project, as does a community or industry partner in the research, as does a participant who engages in the project. Attempting to eliminate bias is artificial, as the nature of reality and the social construction of knowledge means that biases shape every stage of research. However, for a project to be trustworthy, it must ensure that the participants' views are the ones that drive the findings. Researchers need to name and understand their biases to see how their beliefs may affect the study design. Researchers can then, very consciously, create neutral questions that do not presume a particular outcome. For example, if a researcher believes that a particular group of people cannot access health services, the project may focus on barriers and challenges; a neutral research question would explore both barriers and facilitators to access, resulting in a project that is driven by participants' experiences, rather than the researcher's beliefs about the situation. In this way, researchers can consciously examine the power dynamics between themselves and their participants and take steps to balance those dynamics, so that participants feel free to share their views and perspectives without worrying that they will be judged. Similarly, participants holding particular views will then be encouraged to explore the full range of issues relevant to the topic, rather than focusing on their own personal positions. By creating a neutral space for conversation that is shaped by trust, and that allows for multiple perspectives to be shared, researchers can manage bias in ways that lead to the collection of valuable data.

More questions? See #8, #4, and #64.

Can the Findings From Qualitative Research Be Generalized? I've Heard They Can Be Transferable, but I Don't Know the Differences Between These Terms.

Most researchers hope that the results of their projects will be meaningful beyond just the local context and the sample of people they have studied. The value of a project may be judged by one's disciplinary peers based on the implications of the research for a larger population of people or for a broader social context. However, generalizability is not the goal or intention of qualitative research. For a quantitative study to be generalizable, there are specific design requirements that must be met; a sample must be representative of the population, for example, to ensure that the results can be generalized to that larger population. Qualitative projects are designed to be transferable to similar populations, contexts, and settings. For example, a study of boys' reading habits in the United States may be transferable to other, similar countries; however, this transferability will depend on the nature and size of the sample, as well as specific elements of the cultural or social contexts in which the data are gathered.

Researchers must be careful in designing sampling procedures to ensure that the population under study is congruent with the goals of the project. For example, in a study designed to examine children's reading habits, a mix of boys and girls of various ages is needed in order to transfer the findings across all children. If no boys are recruited initially, a researcher will need to engage in purposeful sampling to ensure that boys are included in the study; otherwise, the study's goals would need to change to focus on girls' reading habits, alone. However, transferability of findings is not as simple or straightforward as this would suggest. Deciding whether a project's findings can be transferred across populations, settings, and contexts requires careful investigation of and reflection on the people and issues involved. Many qualitative researchers design various (or large-scale) projects, involving different samples and settings, to determine how far (and in what capacities) their results can transfer to other situations.

More questions? See #1, #15, and #28.

How Do I Ensure That My Study Will Have an Impact on Other Scholars or Practitioners?

Whether a research study has an impact—in academic and/or practice contexts—is, to some degree, outside of the researcher's control. If a study has high academic impact, this may be reflected in the number of people who read and cite the research reports, the number and types of future projects that are developed based on the study's findings, or the number of new opportunities that come to the researcher (such as invitations to give keynote talks). Nonacademic impact also relies on how other individuals or organizations take up and apply the findings of the project. If a hospital is to change its nursing practices, for example, based on the results of a study of patients' experiences in the emergency ward, this impact relies on the organization, professional bodies, individual nurses, and others to implement that change. Even where researchers are involved with community-based co-researchers, there is no guarantee that the findings of the project will lead to a formal change in the community.

There are a number of strategies that researchers can use to ensure that their research is noticed by other scholars and/or practitioners. These strategies can serve as pathways to potential impact and may ensure a broader reach and application of results in academic and nonacademic contexts:

- **Choose research topics that are timely.** Researchers need to have a clear sense of the "hot topics" in their disciplines and/or in practice to ensure that their work is current and addressing issues that will resonate with other scholars and/or practitioners. What are the issues being debated in society? What technological innovations are shaping society? What long-standing areas of investigation continue to capture researchers' and the public's imagination? Focusing the research problem around topics of interest to society, government, and colleagues will ensure that the project is considered timely and relevant and will give the best chance of being "taken up" by others interested in the project's findings.

- **Involve collaborators in research projects.** Working with academic collaborators, especially across disciplines, can enhance the reach of a project's outcomes. Many collaborators can publish in numerous venues and engage a broader network of contacts to disseminate the findings of the work. Working across disciplines can educate other academics about new topic areas, new methodologies, or new practice-related outcomes that they may not have considered previously. Similarly, working with industry partners, community-based organizations, or in specific practice environments can ensure that research topics address practice needs. Involving nonacademic partners may lead to the research results being applied in those specific practice environments, which will also spread the word across the industry-based network that the research has value.

- **Disseminate results in venues where the work will be seen.** When selecting an academic venue for publication, researchers should consider: the disciplinary reputation of journals, conferences, and book publishers; the impact factor and citation history of journals; the number and quality of indexes where journals and conference proceedings are listed; and the breadth of the readership of the venue. Publishing results in the best venues, with the widest readership, will ensure broader reach of the research outcomes. Many media outlets will also review recent publication notices from top venues for interesting projects, which can ensure that the research is given broader public exposure. Researchers should also share their research results through workshops, seminars, newsletter stories, and other strategies, to community-based organizations, government, industry, and professional bodies. This exposure can lead to targeted projects, in future (such as government contracts), as well as implementation of results.

- **Have a public research presence.** In addition to having a presence in academic and practice-based venues, creating a public research profile can enhance the reach of scholars' work. Many researchers are now connected to academic, Web-based profiles (such as Google Scholar, ResearchGate, and Academia.edu) to ensure that other scholars will find them. Uploading publication details, as well as providing commentary about research interests, can ensure that publications are cited and that potential co-investigators are identified. Many organizations (such as universities) also have public "expert directories" on their websites, where researchers can be listed to ensure broader exposure of their work. Journalists, students, community members, government officials, and others also use these sites to see who is conducting research on particular topics. This exposure can lead to future research project invitations, new venues for dissemination, and recruiting of research personnel (such as postdoctoral fellows and Ph.D. students).

More questions? See #2, #3 and #11.

What Are Useful and Practical Approaches to Ensure That I Am Gathering Good Data?

Many qualitative researchers believe that all data are "good" data. This is quite different from quantitative researchers, who hope for statistically significant findings or positive results. As the focus of qualitative research is on participants' views and experiences, or data that emerge during the process, all data gathered have the potential to be valuable and insightful. One of the key measures of qualitative data is whether they address the research questions that have been set out in the project. It is very easy for participants to talk "off topic" or for the researcher to become focused on issues that are not relevant to the study at hand. Although some elements of the research questions may evolve as data emerge, it is important to revisit the research questions regularly to ensure that the data being gathered fit with the topic being explored.

There are also a number of data gathering strategies that can be used to ensure that the data gathered are rich and appropriate for analysis. These strategies include

- **Being a good listener.** Listening well involves "active" listening. Making eye contact, providing positive reinforcement ("Yes, that's interesting"), not interrupting, responding to body language, and other ways of engaging with participants will build rapport and encourage people to open up during data collection.
- **Prompting for details, when needed.** Some participants may speak quickly, with few details. Others may talk, at length, about things that are related—and are not related—to the project. Prompting for more details in a neutral way ("Tell me more about that") or carefully steering the conversation back on topic ("I wanted to go back to something you said earlier") can ensure that data gathered are rich and relevant.
- **Allowing participants to direct the project design.** Emergent design requires that researchers not be too rigid in their original

research plan. If the data are taking the project in a slightly different direction than where the researcher believed the project would go, the participants' views and experiences can shift the focus to a new area. Keeping the research goals on track, while being open to the evolution of the project, will ensure that the data are responsive and relevant to participants' needs and understanding of the issue.

- **Recording data and field notes for later analysis.** It can be difficult to remember all relevant details in the field. Using recording devices (from paper/pens to technological devices) can help to capture additional contextual details during data collection. When engaging with participants directly, using a digital recorder can free the researcher to focus on content (including the need to prompt), rather than struggling to take notes while people talk. However, keeping research notes to jot down points for future analysis or to document details that are not captured on a recording can also be useful.

- **Pilot testing data collection techniques.** Good data arise from good planning, which includes pretesting data collection materials, technology, settings, and so on. Encountering—and resolving—challenges and pitfalls in advance of the core data gathering activity can ensure that the data are sound, rich, and useful for future analysis.

More questions? See #12, #40, and #61.

METHODOLOGIES AND METHODS

What Are the Differences Between Qualitative "Design," "Methodology," and "Method"?

Qualitative researchers use many different terms to describe the nature of their work. At times, these may be used interchangeably (e.g., where a researcher talks about an "approach" to research, when they are referring to the specific "methodology" they have chosen—such as a grounded theory approach/methodology). At other times, one specific word may be used to mean a very specific thing (e.g., when "method" is used to refer to a data collection activity, such as an interview). Unfortunately, researchers cannot always agree on the terminology they use, leaving readers to carefully investigate and define the concepts that are being discussed.

What researchers call the overall "design" of the study is informed by the epistemological stance of the research practice to be undertaken. Some people will simply refer to a "qualitative design," which is a generic term for a range of different conceptual approaches; others will talk about the research following a "constructionist" or "feminist" design to describe the theoretical underpinning of the project. Even if a researcher does not write explicitly about his or her worldview when discussing the project design, relevant details should be provided to outline where the study sits within the varied approaches to research design. Similarly, if a project is a "mixed-methods" study, this will also require different epistemological choices to be made that will inform the mixed approaches to project design.

The "methodology" of the study flows from the overall theoretical or epistemological approach to the design, so there is a fit between the two. In qualitative studies, there are various methodologies researchers use (such as grounded theory, phenomenology, narrative inquiry, or discourse analysis) that direct the design of the study and the choice of specific methods through which data will be gathered and analyzed. The choice of a particular methodology (or methodologies, in larger studies) shapes the research decisions that are made at the implementation stage, including the researcher's writing practices. In a "mixed-methods" study, qualitative and quantitative methodologies may be combined so that the methodologies chosen for each of the designs are congruent at a conceptual level.

The "method" (or methods) that a qualitative researcher chooses for a project is informed by both the epistemological design and the methodology, so there is a conceptual fit at all levels. However, the same method can be used to fit various methodologies; the key difference is the way the method will be enacted to suit the requirements of that methodology. An interview method, for example, can be used in both grounded theory and narrative inquiry methodologies. In grounded theory, for example, a researcher may choose a semistructured interview approach to investigate a range of topics from the participant's perspective. In narrative inquiry, the interview may be unstructured so participants share their personal narratives in their own way. Researchers will often use a range of methods to triangulate the data from various sources. In a "mixed-methods" study, it is not only the methods that are combined (such as qualitative interviews with quantitative questionnaires), but also the theoretical and methodological approaches that inform each of those methods.

More questions? See #5, #7, and #28.

All the Studies I've Read Seem to Use Interviews. What Other Methods Can I Use to Make My Study More Interesting?

Individual and group interviews are two of the most common approaches in qualitative research, since the study design demands that researchers engage with people in some way. Many scholars find "simply talking to people" will provide rich, valuable data that cannot be gathered in any other way. However, no two interviews are the same. The design of the interview (whether semistructured or unstructured) will shape the experience, as will the length of time spent with the participant. Some interviews are conducted in quiet settings, with the researcher and participant facing each other over a recording device; other interviews are conducted while a participant engages in their daily life practices, such as on playgrounds, in school hallways, or as the person undergoes a medical procedure. Some interviews also involve various prompts or activities; talking with participants while they play a video game, for example, can give a rich view of people's experiences when they are "in the moment" of an experience.

In addition to taking a creative approach with the design of interview techniques, there are many other methods researchers can use to engage with participants in interesting ways. Talk-aloud techniques are used to get participants talking while they use search engines; diary methods allow participants to document their views when the researcher is not present in the space; and observing participants as they engage in various activities provides useful data on what people "really do" in a space. Although a one-on-one semistructured interview in a quiet room may seem "less interesting," it may well be the best approach for the research questions. The key question then, when considering how to make the design more "interesting," is whether the innovation in approach is needed for the research problem at hand. In some cases, granting agencies, publishers, thesis supervisory committees, and other external people may pressure a researcher to design using innovative techniques to demonstrate that a project is making methodological advances, in addition to content-based innovations. For these reasons, researchers are wise to seek advice about what might be considered "innovative" within their discipline and design a project that will meet this end goal while addressing the research problem in appropriate ways.

More questions? See #53, #69, and #72.

I Don't Understand the Differences Between Grounded Theory, Phenomenology, Case Study, Ethnography, Narrative Inquiry, and So On. Can I Combine These—Or Choose Not to Use One of These Approaches at All?

All of these are examples of various "methodologies" that can be used in qualitative project designs. The overall design is also informed by an epistemological stance (such as constructionism or feminism) so the methodology selected for a study needs to fit with that overarching view of the study's intent. The methodology drives choices about the methods to be used in the study (such as interviews, focus groups, diaries, etc.), as well as the particular techniques that will be used to implement those methods. Each of these methodologies has its own history, with approaches to design refined over several decades. Grounded theory, for example, dates back to the late 1960s, with modern influences reshaping the approach to study design. Researchers may refer to conducting "classic grounded theory" or "constructivist grounded theory," depending on their worldview and the overall design of the project, so no two grounded theory studies may look exactly alike.

It is important for researchers to read broadly in learning about a new methodology and to consider their own research questions in light of that approach. Even where studies seem to be quite descriptive in nature, and not lending themselves to deep, theoretical approaches, the decision not to apply a particular methodology is a valid choice. In conducting a case-study approach, for example, researchers may choose to follow the tenets of established case-study methodology in their design, or they may refer to the particular setting they have chosen as a "case" but use another methodology within that case to frame their approach to data collection. In the end, the conscious decisions made by researchers in designing their projects and understanding the implications of these choices—particularly where these decisions will affect data collection, analysis, and writing practices—is a key first step in designing research that is of high quality.

More questions? See #5, #28, and #32.

What Kinds of Research Methods Are Appropriate for Talking With People?

Most methods are designed for engaging with people, given the participant-centered focus of qualitative research. Interviews are one of the most commonly used methods in qualitative research, although these vary in their specific designs. Some researchers use semistructured interviews, where the researcher identifies initial questions to guide the flow of the discussion, with the participant redirecting the focus as the conversation unfolds. Other researchers use unstructured interviews, where a single prompting question ("Tell me what it's like to be a nurse") may be the only scripted portion of the design. Some interviews are conducted in formal ways, with the participant and researcher sitting together in a room, with a recording device capturing the discussion. Other interviews are informal, with the individuals talking while engaging in another activity (such as a researcher talking to a senior about nutritional choices while they shop together); in these cases, a researcher may make notes of the discussion later, rather than recording every word.

Focus groups, participant observation, and other methods also involve talking with people directly. In some cases, the discussion is focused on specific topics or issues that are carefully directed by the researcher; in others, dialogue emerges between the researcher and the individual(s) involved, based on the directions that the participant(s) takes the discussion. Other methods (such as participant diaries) can also get people talking to the researcher, despite a bit of distance in the approach. A researcher may want participants to talk about an experience at the time that they are engaging in it, rather than reflecting back on an experience in a traditional interview format. By providing questions to prompt a participant's thinking, or providing texts and images that relate to a specific topic, a researcher can guide the participant's conversation while giving that individual control of what he or she says (or writes) and how he or she says it. Researchers need to give thoughtful consideration to how they want to engage with participants in the study, recognizing that "talking with people" need not be direct and in real time to provide useful and relevant data.

More questions? See #39, #47, and #69.

What Are the Pros and Cons of Conducting Individual Versus Group Interviews?

There are many reasons to use group interviews, instead of individual ones, when conducting qualitative research. Some researchers believe that holding group interviews is more efficient, because a large number of participants can discuss the phenomenon under study at the same time. Similarly, the inclusion of several people, together, can allow people to discuss a number of issues they may not have considered on their own. Many market research techniques find group interviews to be useful for showing clients mock-ups of advertisements or websites, since the group can focus on a number of elements at once and debate the merits of each element with one another. In particular settings (such as schools, hospitals, or large businesses), scheduling group interviews over a few days may also be less disruptive to the organization that is hosting the research team during data collection.

However, there are many challenges in conducting group interviews, so some researchers choose to focus on holding individual meetings. Managing group discussions can be difficult, particularly when some participants dominate the conversation. Scheduling more than one person for a particular timeslot can be challenging; if some participants do not show up at the scheduled time, the entire group may need to be rescheduled. Technology is also an important consideration, as group interviews may require more powerful microphones, two-way glass, video recorders to capture multiple people's faces, and so on. Transcription of group interviews will also take more time, as it can be difficult to distinguish individual voices, particularly when people start to talk at the same time. In projects involving sensitive topics, group interviews may not be appropriate, as individuals may not feel comfortable discussing these topics in front of other people.

Researchers need to make choices about method selection and participant recruitment that suit the research questions being addressed, as well as logistics involved in data collection. At times, the researcher's preference may not suit the data collection site, particularly when other organizations are involved. Researchers must consider the topic, timing, costs, logistics, and other issues when making their decision, including participants' own needs and preferences.

More questions? See #12, #13, and #38.

I Want to Observe What People Are Doing, But I Don't Want Them to Know That I'm Watching. Can I Do That?

Qualitative researchers, who want to examine individuals' activities in natural settings and without influencing those activities, use covert observation to gather data. Researchers may walk through a public park to see how people use technology in these spaces. Or, they may observe people's behavior when lining up to enter a movie theater. In some cases, researchers will set up videos to record activities in pubic spaces; in others, they will take notes in the field to document what they see. As with all methods selected for use in qualitative studies, the choice of observational approach will depend on the research problem and the methodology informing the study, as well as logistics (e.g., how best to document what is happening given the layout of the space).

However, covert observation also carries a number of ethics implications that are unique to this approach. In some jurisdictions, for example, researchers may not need to go through formal ethics review to conduct covert observation in public spaces. As this method does not involve direct interaction with the people observed, and as there is often no expectation of privacy in a public space, researchers may be able to gather data freely in these environments. However, defining a "public" space can be challenging; for example, although many people see shopping malls as public space, these are actually private, corporate environments, so conducting this type of research may be challenging. Similarly, deciding how to operationalize "observation" may not be that clear; for example, does this allow a researcher to document things that are overheard in the space or only what is seen? Research ethics boards can provide advice to researchers about how best to use covert approaches, particularly the stage at which ethics review would be required.

More questions? See #16, #68, and #71.

How Can I Use Documents in My Qualitative Study?

There are many different ways to use documents in qualitative research, beyond the typical use of these materials for the literature review and/or to inform the design of the project. Documents can be used as the sole focus for data collection and analysis, or they may be used as tools within another data collection method to complement that approach. It is important to first consider what is meant by the term "document," as a text can take many forms; a document may be an excerpt of a poem, a publication, a website, or another form of textual material. A document may also be a photograph, a map, a bar graph, a comic strip, or another style of visual representation of knowledge. In some cases, a document may refer to a multimedia file (such as an audio recording or a film) or a physical entity (such as a sculpture or a technological device). These documents may be external to the project, where the researcher locates a text and brings it into the data collection or analysis, or they may be internal products of the research (such as interview transcripts).

The following are some examples of the various ways documents are used in qualitative research:

- **As the focus of the analysis.** Qualitative researchers can analyze documents, in their own right, using various content analysis approaches. Discourse analysis, for example, may be used to explore the social construction of the concept of poverty in government policy documents. Qualitative content analysis may be used to examine common themes or patterns in Twitter posts during a flood emergency. In an observational study, for example, ads on the walls of hospital waiting rooms may form part of the analysis, in addition to data gathered while observing individuals in the space. In all of these cases, the documents themselves are the focus of the investigation.

- **As prompts to participants during data collection.** Documents can also be used in interviews, focus groups, or other data collection methods to prompt participants to engage in conversation.

A mock-up of a website design, for example, can be shown to people to get their views on navigation, design aesthetics, content, or other elements of the site. Photographs of the war may prompt retired soldiers to revisit their time in service and reflect on specific events. Researchers may collect and bring documents to the data collection sessions, or participants may be asked to bring materials relevant to the topic for discussion purposes. In some cases, the documents themselves may become part of the dataset, to be analyzed alongside the interview or focus group results.

- **As creative outcomes of data collection.** Researchers may also ask participants to engage in a creative activity as part of a study, where the output of that activity becomes part of the dataset. A young child, for example, may be asked to draw a picture of his or her friends and family; the picture may serve as a prompt for an interview but may also become a focus of analysis in its own right. University students may be asked to keep diaries of their study habits so that they can document details "in the moment," which the researcher can review at a later stage. Seniors may be given audio recorders and asked to document their nutrition choices throughout each day, over several weeks, which can then be discussed during future interviews with the research team.

More questions? See #9, #21, and #71.

I've Heard That There Are Some Interesting Visual Methods That I Can Use—What Are They?

There are many different visual methods that researchers can use in their projects during data collection. These fall into two main areas:

1. **Researcher-generated visual methods.** Researchers often use visuals as data sources, as well as to enhance other methods (such as interviews). Here, the visuals are identified and managed by the research team, rather than the participants. Examples include:

   a. **Textual methods.** Researchers gather visuals (such as magazine advertisements) to use as data sources in document analysis. Here, analysis is focused on the document itself; the document may also be used as part of a task-based method with participants (e.g., where the ads are discussed during interviews) or may stand alone as a data source.

   b. **Photographic methods.** Researchers use still or video cameras to document a setting, participants, activities, and so on, for later data analysis and writing. Images and clips may be used in dissemination (e.g., as part of a conference presentation, in a journal article, or the release of a documentary on the issue).

   c. **Task-based methods.** Researchers ask participants to search for information on a computer, to look at advertisements in a magazine, or to comment on mock-ups of a design. The materials are gathered or created by the research team and provided to the participants for discussion, in interviews, focus groups, diary responses, and so on.

2. **Participant-generated visual methods.** Researchers also ask participants to create or identify visuals during data collection. These may be used alongside other (researcher-generated) methods such

as interviews or focus groups. However, the participant has control over the data collection process by deciding what visuals to include and/or create.

a. **Textual methods.** Participants provide documents (such as family photographs) to the research team, which form part of the dataset for analysis.

b. **Photographic methods.** Participants use still or video cameras to document their experiences. The research team may provide equipment and advice about the types of information to gather, but the participant decides on the process and content of data collection.

c. **Task-based methods.** Participants draw images, cut images from magazines, create Web pages, write poems, or engage in other creative activities during data collection.

More questions? See #9, #11, and #47.

In My Discipline We Conduct a Lot of Systematic Reviews of the Literature. Is It Possible to Do a Qualitative Systematic Review?

Systematic reviews emerged in the health sciences disciplines as a way to evaluate published research by measuring studies against an established "gold standard" of evidence. In these reviews, experiments using randomized controlled designs (as are used in studies of new medications, for example) are at the top of the hierarchy of evidence; studies using other project designs are ranked further down the list, with single cases or "anecdotal" evidence presented at the bottom of the list. Systematic reviews provide comprehensive assessments of the best evidence to date, which can then be applied in practice.

The systematic review process cannot be easily modified for assessing qualitative research projects. Often, the "gold standard" of evidence excludes qualitative research entirely; when qualitative research practices are mentioned, they appear at the bottom of the hierarchy. Unfortunately, to readers who are unfamiliar with qualitative practices, this may cause them to believe (inappropriately!) that qualitative research is not sound and does not provide useful evidence on which to make decisions.

Qualitative research can be assessed through systematic review processes; however, the "gold standard" of what is considered the "best evidence" must change to reflect qualitative practices. Although some researchers (especially in health disciplines) have started to develop such approaches, there is no agreement on what the gold standard might be in this area. In part, this is due to the nature of qualitative inquiry itself. For example, as there are various approaches to grounded theory methodology, establishing a single, standard assessment of the evidence produced in grounded theory studies is not appropriate. Also, a "gold standard" implies a single approach to reality, which is opposed to the relative, constructionist view of reality that informs most qualitative designs. For individuals in the health sciences, in particular, where systematic reviews are held in high regard, the integration of qualitative evidence in these models will continue to be a key issue in the years to come.

More questions? See #2, #3, and #7.

PART 6

MIXED-METHODS RESEARCH INVOLVING QUALITATIVE APPROACHES

I've Heard That Qualitative Research Is Only Useful as a First, Exploratory Step to Designing a Quantitative Project—Is That True?

In some cases, qualitative research is used as a preliminary step to the design of quantitative projects. Focus groups may be held to explore the range and style of questions to be asked on a questionnaire. Individual interviews may be conducted across a large geographic area to ensure that a quantitative design captures the range of issues across various rural and urban contexts. In these types of projects, qualitative methods serve a very functional role; they provide qualitative data to guide quantitative methods design, without consideration for the needs of a full qualitative paradigm design. For this reason, the researchers may use only one method (without any triangulation), they may use smaller sample sizes than what would be required for qualitative transferability, and they may not analyze and publish the results. Rather, this is seen as a preliminary stage in quantitative design work, serving more like a pilot project for the ultimate design than a research project in its own right.

Given the many decades of qualitative research that has been conducted across disciplines, it would not be fair to say that qualitative projects are "only" useful when they lead to quantitative design. This belief may be prevalent in some disciplines, especially those that privilege quantitative, experimental, or clinical designs. Unfortunately, this belief tends to be grounded in ignorance of the range of possibilities afforded by qualitative research practices. Where researchers have not received any education or training in qualitative research, or where they have only seen this type of research being used as a preliminary step to quantitative design, it is understandable that these individuals will have a very limited view of qualitative research. Where individuals are educated in the qualitative paradigm and see how various methods can be used together to gather rich and robust data for analysis, they begin to see that the possibilities within the qualitative approach far outweigh using a single technique to inform another design.

More questions? See #1, #29, and #30.

How Can Qualitative Research Complement a Quantitative Study?

Qualitative research can be used to complement quantitative studies, just as quantitative research can complement qualitative projects. Qualitative projects are designed to dig deeply into an issue; they drill down into what it means to experience a phenomenon, providing data that illuminate that experience. Quantitative projects are designed to look broadly across a phenomenon; they gaze at a phenomenon at a surface level, providing data that demonstrate the reach and influence of an issue. When these two approaches are combined, a researcher can get the best of both worlds in their data collection and analysis.

For example, a quantitative project might be designed to explore health care practitioners' views on emergency room care for young children. A nationwide questionnaire of nurses, physicians, and pharmacists gathers quantitative data from a large sample of health care practitioners working in various types of hospitals, in rural and urban communities. The data present a picture of the demographics of these health care practitioners (their ages, number of years in the workforce, education), as well as data about their patients' symptoms, diagnoses, number of hours spent in the emergency ward, and other data that can be used for statistical analyses.

However, this questionnaire cannot provide an in-depth view of what it is like to work in the emergency room, caring for young children. A qualitative study can be designed to explore the processes at work in the emergency unit. Interviews with nurses, physicians, and pharmacists can delve into the issues they face in caring for these young children. Observations of the unit can illuminate the nature of that care by documenting the various processes at work, simultaneously, on the unit. Methods aimed at patients, as well, can investigate the issue from another perspective. In this way, a researcher can triangulate across both methods and populations to gather a more complete picture of what it means to experience emergency care in this environment.

These qualitative data can also lead the researcher to develop additional quantitative approaches, which are informed by the analysis of initial quantitative and qualitative data. A questionnaire aimed at patients, for example, can then provide national data for many of the experiences identified during qualitative analysis as being important to children and their families in the emergency ward. In this way, quantitative and qualitative approaches can complement and inform each other and provide a rich (deep and broad) picture of the experience.

More questions? See #8, #55, and #66.

Which Do I Do First—The Qualitative Component of the Study or the Quantitative Component?

Deciding whether to conduct a qualitative component before a quantitative component—or vice versa—is an important decision to make, based on the goals of the study. However, there is no single, correct answer to this question. In fact, another alternative is to conduct both components at the same time so that the results from each can guide data collection and analysis practices. There are a number of considerations to make when choosing the ideal timing of qualitative and quantitative phases of a project, including

- **Research goals.** If the design of a quantitative questionnaire depends on the completion of a qualitative focus group, then the research design predetermines the order of activities. If these two methods are to be used, but the questions to be asked of participants in both the questionnaire and the focus group can be designed independently, then either approach may come first in the design. Either way, it is vital that research team members with appropriate expertise are available to support the phases of the project, whatever the timing of each phase.
- **Participants' needs.** If the quantitative component of a study (such as an online questionnaire) can be completed whenever the participant chooses, but the qualitative component (such as an in-person focus group) is dependent on their availability, as well as the schedules of other participants, it may make sense to run the qualitative component first, as it may take more time to plan. Considering the participants' needs when designing the order of study components may ensure quicker and easier recruitment, as well as leaving enough time for data collection in the research site.
- **Money, time, and other logistics.** If a qualitative component of a study requires travel, on-site data collection, or other considerations that will affect the cost and duration of a project, the timing of the

project may depend on time of year, location, size of research team, and other issues. Balancing the project's goals with participants' needs, while keeping an eye on the budget and timing of the project, are key to successful project phase management.

More questions? See #7, #28, and #55.

I Have Included Some Open-Ended Questions Alongside the Closed-Response Items on My Survey/Questionnaire. Am I Conducting Qualitative Research?

Although open-ended questions on a questionnaire will provide qualitative data, this approach does not constitute a qualitative research design. If this is the only qualitative component of a quantitative study design, the project cannot be said to be using a mixed-methods design, either. Qualitative research reflects a qualitative paradigm, where the design is informed by an epistemological worldview that privileges meaning-focused investigations of human experience.

Qualitative data on a questionnaire provide concrete textual responses that can complement statistical data; however, these qualitative data are typically analyzed in ways that reduce the text to word frequency counts or to provide a few quotes to support the statistical analyses. The focus in these investigations is on the quantitative paradigm, where sampling procedures, statistical tests, and writing styles in publications reflect that paradigm. The inclusion of questions designed to gather qualitative data does not change the overall nature of the study.

More questions? See #5, #7, and #8.

Is It Better to Bring a Qualitative Researcher Onto My Team, or Should I Try to Do the Qualitative Research Myself?

As with all research practices, qualitative research requires special training and experience to become expert in its application. Even where an individual has completed doctoral work or gained research experience working on teams alongside qualitative experts, learning the nuances of particular methodologies and methods can take several years, across multiple projects. For researchers who are not familiar with qualitative approaches, the methods may look deceptively easy; simply "talking to people" about their opinions, just "watching" people in public spaces, or simply "reading a text for deeper meaning" may appear to be the kinds of activities that people do all the time. However, the design, implementation, and analysis of qualitative projects can be very challenging work. It requires researchers to apply specialized knowledge of the approaches in the moment to adjust research practices as the project evolves. Once data are gathered, the analysis process can take several weeks or months of intense thematic review and theorizing.

For these reasons, a team-based project that includes a qualitative component is best designed with a qualitative researcher involved from the beginning of the project. However, not all qualitative researchers are alike. Individual scholars have expertise in particular methods, with specific populations and settings, or other specialized areas of focus. Their approach to research design, as well as their epistemological worldview, will be particular, and may or may not suit the project design that the team envisions. Despite the challenges involved in finding a team member who will be a good fit for the project, doing so is a better time investment than conducting qualitative research yourself, without any training or experience with the approach. External peer reviewers (whether with granting agencies or journal publishers) will also look favorably on qualitative expertise embedded in the team; a lack of appropriate expertise about research practices is readily apparent in writing about the work, which may result in negative assessments during peer review.

More questions? See #5, #12, and #69.

I've Only Ever Used Quantitative Designs, but I Want to Use Qualitative Approaches Now—What Are the Key Issues I Need to Consider and How Can I Learn More About Them?

Deciding to use qualitative approaches in study design when one's training, education, and prior experience is solely informed by quantitative practices is a major decision. In some ways, researchers need to go "back to basics" in their thinking about research design when making this move. Researchers will need to carefully review their ontological and epistemological stances, including how these have shaped their work in the past, in order to design appropriate qualitative studies. Reviewing key qualitative design texts in light of one's worldview will be an important step in refocusing attention from an existing, quantitative mindset. Unlike an individual with no research training (who may not, for example, understand how research is conducted or know the basic tenets of ethical research practice), a quantitative researcher has learned a number of skills and approaches that are shaped by a particular conceptual worldview. This means that researchers will need to make a significant paradigm shift in their thinking, as well as their research practices, in order to be successful when engaging in qualitative research.

The first step in making the transition to qualitative research is to understand that the nature of this research approach is conceptually different from quantitative research. Where quantitative projects go broad and are driven by a desire for generalization and statistical significance, qualitative projects go deep and are driven by a desire to understand meaning and process in ways that can be transferable across groups. Quantitative researchers need to reconsider their approaches to sample size, case selection, data analysis, writing, and many other design decisions that shape the conduct of the research. As quantitative research sits on the positivist end of the spectrum, scholars' own worldviews may also be put into question, given that qualitative research tends toward constructionist understandings of reality.

One of the best starting places is to partner with a qualitative research expert so that a researcher who is making the transition from quantitative can learn from a colleague in an apprentice-style relationship. Although there are also many workshops and seminars offered, and hundreds of publications and websites designed to guide qualitative research practice, personal mentoring from a scholar with relevant expertise will ensure that the transition is smooth. Given that learning any research practice can take years, across multiple projects, building strong collaborative relationships with qualitative colleagues can ensure that quantitative researchers can gain the knowledge and skills necessary to engage in quality work.

More questions? See #1, #7, and #12.

PART 7

COLLECTING QUALITATIVE DATA

How Do I Conduct a Pilot Study for My Qualitative Research Project?

A pilot study is a small-scale phase of a larger project, which is designed to test the approaches that will be used in the final study. Often, pilot studies are rolled into the study design and discussed in the ethics application. If the pilot phase is successful, results may be rolled into the full dataset; however, if there are problems with the pilot, the researcher has time to make changes (such as purchasing new equipment or revising the wording of a question) before starting the full data collection period.

Pilot studies allow researchers to

- **Practice and refine research instruments.** One of the most important outcomes of a pilot study is that a researcher gains a clear understanding of how an interview guide, focus group discussion guide, content analysis schema, or other data collection instrument will "work" in the field. Testing these instruments helps to refine the questions so the data collection period that follows will be the best it can be.
- **Ensure that a participant type is a fit for the study.** The pilot phase can also confirm whether the types of participants a researcher has chosen really can provide data that address the goals of the study. For example, a researcher may begin by recruiting a broad range of ages into a study of "young children." By conducting a pilot phase, the researcher may find that a specific age group (such as teens) is the best one to target for the types of data to be gathered. In this way, the recruiting process can be adjusted to focus on the specific group, providing richer and more relevant data during the full data collection period than would have been possible with the original participant age range.
- **Explore a new research site.** Often, researchers are gathering data in settings they have not previously encountered. By entering the space during a pilot phase, the researcher can assess the layout, lighting, traffic flows, and other issues relevant to data collection.

Interviewing people in a coffee shop, for example, may be too loud for data collection, whereas interviewing people in a quiet space may cause the sound to echo, making it difficult to have a confidential conversation. Conducting observational work on a street may prove difficult due to physical obstructions or other unforeseen challenges. By gathering pilot data, at various times of day and in various locations, the researcher will be able to see if there are any particular issues that need to be addressed prior to starting full data collection.

- **Test equipment.** Researchers often face technical issues when conducting research. Batteries may fail, websites may not load, or a room may not have an electrical outlet to plug in a computer. By testing equipment in advance, during a pilot phase, a researcher will become more comfortable with the technology, reducing the chance of human error (such as not hitting the record button on a video camera). Although some technical details can be tested without participants present, running through a few full-length sessions will provide an opportunity to assess battery life, download speeds for testing websites, and determine whether a recorder can pick up a soft voice. Having a backup plan (such as providing print copies of documents to review with participants, rather than relying on live websites) can also reduce the chances of technical failures during data collection.

- **Assess how long data collection will take to complete.** Researchers try to estimate the length of data collection sessions in advance, when designing projects and completing ethics review applications. Advice from colleagues, past experience, and general guidance from research methods text can provide some sense of how long an individual data collection session will take to complete. However, until a researcher tests the process with a sample of participants, it is often impossible to know what will be realistic given the scope of the topic and the nature of participants' experiences. Although individual sessions may vary, running a few sessions will give a researcher a clear sense of the time range he or she may need to devote to the process.

- **Feel more at ease with the project design.** Researchers are often nervous before they start a new project, particularly when the project involves new equipment, new settings, or significant financial and time commitments. A pilot phase can put the researcher's mind at ease, demonstrating that the research instruments are well designed, that the amount of time allocated for data collection is realistic, and that the researcher is comfortable with the project design he or she has crafted. Even if the pilot phase does not identify any problems, the relief that this will bring is well worth the time investment!

- **Provide initial evidence/publications to support future project development work.** Some researchers use pilot phases of the work very strategically to gather initial data as a "proof of concept" for future project development work. By designing and implementing a small-scale study a few months (or more) prior to a grant-funding application deadline, researchers can demonstrate the value of the work. Pilot data may be publishable, depending on sample sizes, which will establish that the work is viable and ongoing.

- **Test relationships with new co-investigators or new community/industry partners.** When researchers embark on new relationships, whether with colleagues or with community-based research partners, it can be a good idea to design a small-scale study to test the research relationships. This can be a "low-stakes" commitment on the part of both the researcher and the potential partner, as the timeframes are often short and the amount of money and time spent is typically quite small. The success of team-based research hinges on productive working relationships, so researchers may do best to build a larger project out of something small as a way to establish the foundation for future success.

More questions? See #35, 45, and #55.

My Colleague Says That We Need to Be Unobtrusive When Gathering Data—What Does That Mean?

Qualitative researchers often want to "be part of the furniture" when they are gathering data for their studies. If they are observing activities in the field—whether watching children on a playground or listening to executives in a boardroom meeting—the goal is to blend into the background of the environment so as not to disrupt the activities underway. Qualitative data are often gathered in these types of naturalistic settings as the people being studied go about their everyday lives. Researchers want to be sure that they are collecting data on individuals' spontaneous, natural activities, rather than data that result from being studied—what is known as the "observer effect." In some cases (i.e., covert studies), projects are designed so the individuals being studied are not even aware that the research is taking place; hidden cameras may capture the activity for later analysis, or a researcher may walk through a space to observe the activity and take notes only after leaving the field. In these cases, the researcher is fully unobtrusive—that is, not intruding in the activity and not noticeable to the individuals being studied.

At the other end of the spectrum, the researcher may be fully embedded as a participant in the activity, engaging openly and prominently with the participants. In these cases, participants know who the researcher is, they see the researcher gathering data, and they talk with the researcher; the researcher is fully obtrusive, acknowledging his or her influence on the participants and using that stance to advantage in data gathering and analysis. For example, by embracing the role of participant, a researcher may be able to ask questions that are informed by his or her own experience of the event, and not just as an outsider looking into the setting. This engagement can build trust and rapport with participants, allowing the researcher to gather data that would otherwise be unavailable for analysis.

In the middle of these two ends of the spectrum are many shades of gray—that is, where a researcher is visible and known to the participants but is also trying to gather data without influencing the natural activities or responses of the people being studied. Being unobtrusive in these situations can be difficult, particularly in studies using active techniques of engagement (e.g., interviewing participants, video recording activities). Of course, it is difficult to be fully unobtrusive; however, there are a number of data gathering techniques that researchers use to maintain a level of unobtrusiveness, even while being prominent in the research space:

- Dressing in clothing similar to the group under study to blend into the crowd more easily;
- Using small devices to record data (e.g., small notebooks, lapel microphones), which are not as noticeable to participants;
- Using devices that are commonly seen in the participants' daily lives (e.g., recording on a smartphone, when these devices are used by the people under study);
- Positioning devices to the side of the activity (e.g., on the edge of the table, rather than in the center) so that they are not the focus of the participant's attention;
- Engaging in conversational dialogue with participants (e.g., memorizing interview questions, taking few notes) so as not to distract the participant; and
- Using active listening techniques (e.g., making eye contact, not interrupting, allowing silence) to ensure that participants are the focus of the engagement, rather than the recording devices.

More questions? See #16, #45, and #51.

Can I Hire Someone to Do All of the Data Collection?

Many qualitative researchers hire staff to help with data collection and other phases of the research. In large, multi-site projects, for example, the work may not be possible without the support of a team of paid research assistants, technicians, or professional researchers. One of the main challenges for qualitative researchers, however, is that data analysis occurs *alongside* data collection; for this reason, researchers need to be involved in all phases of the research work to reflect on and guide the work of hired staff so that data collection and analysis are implemented appropriately. Even where data collection and analysis are designed to be discrete phases, the nature of the work requires reflection, documentation, and initial analysis at the earliest phases of data collection.

When hiring staff, researchers must understand the nature of the work and advise staff on appropriate strategies for documenting decisions made in the field. A hired interviewer, for example, must have a clear understanding of the project goals to be able to make adjustments to the interview guide in the moment. A team of interviewers will need to share notes and decisions regularly, in the field, so that adjustments are made across the board. A hired transcriptionist is paid to transform audio-recordings into verbatim textual scripts of the interaction and can do this very quickly alongside data collection. However, the initial analysis that a researcher would complete while engaging in transcription will be lost, despite the quick turnaround time for completing the transcripts. Similarly, if the transcriptionist has not completed the interview, specific details (such as acronyms) may not be accurately recorded in the transcribed documentation.

Despite these limitations, there is no doubt that hiring people to help with data collection is a useful and appropriate strategy in many projects. Researchers need to understand these limitations and they need to develop contingency plans to manage the challenges that hired staff present. These include

- **Training of hired staff.** Data collection and analysis work are complex activities that require thoughtful consideration of the research goals throughout the implementation of the study. Staff must be aware of the project's goals and in constant connection with the research team to ensure that everyone is aware of shifts in focus or other emergent issues as the study unfolds. Training staff in the use of particular methods (e.g., how to build rapport during an interview), as well as the identification of key analytical issues (e.g., when an emergent theme requires a change to the interview guide) will take time and needs to be ongoing throughout the project.

- **Data checking of research materials.** The research team needs to review transcripts, field notes, and other materials gathered during data collection and analysis to ensure that these documents fully reflect the scope and intention of the research activities. Members of the research team should review the recordings and the textual transcripts to check data accuracy and completeness. Where hired staff is documenting details in the field, making initial analysis notes, or reviewing relevant literature to inform analysis, the research team needs to review these materials and discuss how the staff is conceptualizing the project to ensure that everyone is using a similar approach to documentation.

- **Regular check-ins with the team as part of project management.** Sound project management skills on the part of the researcher are paramount in projects involving hired staff, particularly when the research team is large, distributed across distances, and interdisciplinary. Conducting regular formal meetings, as well as informal check-ins on progress, can ensure that the research team is "on the same page" as project decisions are made in the field.

More questions? See #14, #16, and #81.

What Does It Mean to Be "Neutral" When I'm Gathering My Data?

Qualitative researchers understand that everyone brings their personal views, biases, and orientations along with them when conducting research. Researchers choose topics that interest them, often with groups of people with whom they work closely. In order to gather data that reflect participants' views, projects are designed so that the researcher can maintain a neutral stance.

When the research questions are identified, for example, a researcher writes the questions using neutral language so that the research design does not presume a particular outcome. If the researcher writes, "What barriers do women experience in pursuing careers in engineering?" the question presumes that barriers exist. If the research question says, instead, "What are women's experiences in pursuing careers in engineering?" there is room for the participants to explore alternatives to a barrier-focused reality. The question "What barriers and/or facilitators do women experience in pursuing careers in engineering?" can focus the researcher's attention on both the negative and positive experiences, without presuming that either is the case for the participants. However, this type of wording can lead to a binary assessment of the positives and negatives, which may oversimplify the women's experiences. Even where the existing research literature points to a history of barriers, qualitative researchers are careful to leave room to "be surprised" in the study design. They achieve this by ensuring that neutrality shapes the approach to the project.

At the time of data collection, researchers must also be careful to maintain a neutral stance. When designing interview questions or asking people to write diary entries about their experiences, for example, a researcher will be careful to prompt the participant with questions that are designed to be neutral. Asking a participant, "Did you feel bad when that happened?" may produce a very different outcome than asking, "How did you feel when that happened?" Taking a neutral stance in data collection is particularly important when a researcher is engaging with participants who do not share the researcher's own perspective on an issue. For example, if a researcher believes in marriage equality but is interviewing participants who believe marriage is between a man and a woman only, a neutral stance will allow the participants' views to be the focus of data collection.

Of course, part of maintaining a neutral stance also depends on the researcher's demeanor during data collection. Being careful not to show surprise, shock, disgust, or other emotions that may appear to be judging participants when they are sharing their personal views is an important part of maintaining neutrality during data collection. This allows participants to feel at ease during data collection so that they will be frank and open in choosing what to share with the researcher.

More questions? See #40, #41, and #69.

What Does "Fieldwork" Involve in a Qualitative Project?

The "fields" where qualitative research is conducted are very diverse. Generally, when people talk about being "in the field," they mean that they are engaging in data collection and analysis activities outside of the normal workspace (such as their personal office). The field may be a coffee shop, a hospital waiting room, a preschool classroom, a public park, or many other contexts in which research is conducted. Even booking an interview space down the hall from one's own office can be considered a "field" of sorts, since it is away from the everyday space that the researcher inhabits. In digital research, however, it is also possible to be "in the field" even while sitting at one's own desk. If researchers are engaged in data collection and analysis work on a Listserv, for example, they may see themselves in a virtual research "field." Even though the tool may be the same as the one they use for checking e-mail, marking assignments, or doing other work as part of their regular job, entering a research mindset that is in "data gathering mode" may be viewed as its own research field.

Activities in the research field may be very similar to what researchers do when they are not in the field. Typing on a keyboard, note taking, talking, thinking, using recording devices, reading, searching online, and other activities are all part of qualitative fieldwork. Although the term "fieldwork" brings to mind images of digging in dirt (in archaeology) or communing with nature (in agriculture), qualitative fieldwork often involves sitting in chairs, working on a computer, watching people, listening, and other reflective activities. Although some research approaches involve hands-on work with participants (such as showing people advertisements to gauge their perspectives), other approaches are quiet and thoughtful (such as observing children at play). The nature of fieldwork varies with each project but often looks very much like what researchers do in their everyday lives. The difference is often what is going on inside the minds of the researchers, which is where the real digging and communing happens.

More questions? See #31, #76, and #77.

What Does It Mean to Gather "Rich Data"?

Qualitative researchers use the term "rich data" to describe the plentiful and deep nature of the data gathered in their studies. In addition to capturing the facts, by describing something that happened ("I went to the public library"), naming a feeling ("I was frightened"), or stating a belief ("Young children should spend more time outdoors"), participants provide thick, highly descriptive data that can be analyzed in many different ways. Participants describing when they felt frightened may describe the incident itself, they may relate that to other times they have felt the same way, and they may talk about how they overcame that feeling. The discussion of one particular feeling, incident, or belief may last for several minutes, or it may be the central point of discussion for hours, over multiple data collection sessions. Further, that particular topic may also be explored with other people, in other texts, or by engaging the participant in other forms of data collection (such as drawing a picture that represents their feelings). The dataset provides many possible quotes that can be used in qualitative writing, and, when compared to other participants' narratives or data drawn from other sources, the depth and richness of the dataset is compounded. For this reason, qualitative analysis can take a very long time, and it can result in multiple publications examining various themes. Rich data provide for rich analyses and rich approaches to writing, where participants' perspectives and voices provide substantial points of evidence to shape and support the researcher's interpretation of the data.

More questions? See #56, #89, and #96.

Do I Have to Transcribe All of My Interview Data or Can I Simply Transcribe a Few Quotes When I Need Them?

Ideally, qualitative researchers will transcribe all of their data themselves, at the time the data are collected. The reflection and initial analyses that occur when a researcher transcribes the data allow adjustments to be made to interview questions, observational techniques, or other data collection approaches as part of emergent design. This is an important part of initial data analysis and will inform the writing process. By replaying recordings in the transcription process, a researcher can revisit the key issues raised by participants and begin to document themes and potential codes to inform the later phases of analysis. Typically, researchers will schedule data collection at appropriate intervals (holding focus group interviews over several weeks, for example) to allow for transcription time and adjustments to the data collection and analysis process.

However, all qualitative researchers need to make pragmatic choices about how transcription will be done and at what stage of project implementation. If a researcher must balance data collection and analysis with other duties (such as teaching and service work), they may decide to hire a research assistant to help with transcription. However, training novice assistants and finding time to debrief to ensure that data collection practices are modified appropriately can extend the time for project completion. If the budget allows, a researcher may also hire a professional transcription service, which can speed the process and allow the researcher to review the recordings and make data collection decisions quickly. Participants' needs, particularly where data collection is being conducted in a setting where the timing cannot be fully controlled by the researcher, may also affect the timing and process of transcription. For example, if data collection must be completed in a more compressed timeframe than first planned, transcription may need to wait until after the data are gathered. In these cases, researchers may rely on field notes to adjust data collection practices (where needed) and complete transcription at a later stage.

At times, the need for selective transcription may be driven by situations that are beyond the researcher's control. For example, a call for papers for a conference or special issue of a journal may have a short deadline; for the researcher to complete a paper on time, he or she may need to conduct analysis from the audio or video recordings and transcribe selected quotes only for use in the publication. However, many researchers are now starting to see the value of this type of selective transcription for more than just "unusual" or "emergency" situations. Most qualitative data analysis software packages now allow researchers to import audio or video files, which can be coded directly in the system. This reduces the need for full transcription but also allows the researcher to view participants' comments within the broader context in which data were gathered.

More questions? See #13, #81, and #96.

What Are the Pros and Cons of Audio or Video Recording My Participants?

Qualitative researchers often record their engagement with participants to provide a record of data collection sessions that can be used for analysis. Although the decision to use audio versus video recordings will vary depending on the study design, having an accurate record of the data collection period can provide a number of benefits to the researcher. However, these potential benefits must be balanced against the downsides of recording so researchers ensure that they are making the best possible choice given the nature of the study design, as well as considering participants' needs. The following are some of the pros and cons of using recording devices in data collection:

Benefits of Using Recording Devices

- Provide accurate records of data gathered (e.g., video recording of participants engaged in an activity);
- Participants' quotes can be transcribed verbatim for use in analysis and in publications;
- Recorded data may be given to research assistants or professional staff for transcription; and
- Recorded files can be uploaded into specialized software for coding and analysis purposes.

Challenges of Using Recording Devices

- Only capture some data (i.e., what can be viewed in the camera's frame), so important contextual data may be lost;
- Technical failures can occur, resulting in lost data;
- Participants may be uncomfortable in the presence of the recorder and not share information with the researcher;

- Researcher field notes or other data sources are needed to capture contextual details; and
- Recording devices and analysis software require specialized training for effective use.

More questions? See #12, #45, and #62.

Qualitative Research Seems to Involve a Lot of Talking to People. Sounds Easy—So What Issues Should I Expect if I'm Doing Formal or Informal Interviews With Individuals or Groups?

Although people talk to each other every day, the type of talking that occurs in a research setting is far more complex and very demanding on the part of both researchers and participants. A researcher will be asking questions of the participant, guided not only by an interview guide (either in paper form or one they have memorized), but also by the responses of the person they are interviewing. Depending on what a participant says in the interview, the researcher must guide the conversation in various ways to ensure that the process gathers data relevant to the topic being studied. At the same time, a researcher may be walking through a space with the participant and observing details of that environment; the interview may be conducted while walking through the participant's job site, or while the person uses a computer. The researcher needs to reflect on relevant details in the environment and draw upon these details in shaping the next questions to be asked.

In a group interview setting, the cognitive load can be much higher for the researcher. Managing group members' personalities to ensure that everyone's voice is heard requires particular skills and patience. Keeping the conversation on topic, showing materials to the group to prompt discussion, and ensuring that the interview does not go over-time can take a great deal of practice. If the participant group has particular needs (such as young children who may not sit still for very long), the researcher will also need to be sensitive to these and flexible during the data collection process.

Of course, during the interview, the researcher may also be taking notes, checking that an audio recorder is working, or quietly directing a research assistant to change the angle of a camera. The process of qualitative interviewing is one where multitasking is the norm. Balancing the intellectual work of question development, alongside the mundane activities of adjusting a tripod angle, is part of the normal work of a qualitative researcher. The process of obtaining informed consent for participation may also need to be negotiated during the interview itself, particularly where sensitive topics become the focus of the discussion. In addition, once the interview has ended, the researcher must be sure to document field notes of the experience to note unusual issues that arose or to note changes that need to be made to the interview guide. The cognitive load of balancing these various activities cannot be understated. Researchers may only be able to conduct one or two brief interviews in a day, or just several interviews during a week, given the intellectual and logistical work involved.

More questions? See #13, #64, and #68.

Do I Have to Work With My Participants in Person, or Can I Use the Internet (or Other Tools) to Gather Data at a Distance?

Increasingly, researchers are using many technological tools to gather data at a distance from their participants. Although telephones have been used for decades for qualitative interviewing, researchers often raised concerns about the lack of personal connection afforded by this technology when engaging with participants. Newer technologies (such as Skype) allow qualitative researchers to mirror in-person interviewing techniques. This helps to build rapport with participants and also provides ways to show people materials or share links to websites, which may be a key part of an interview design. High-speed Internet now allows for better resolution and more reliable connections than were possible previously, so these approaches are considered quite useful for project design.

Technology can also be used to engage participants in offline activities, such as writing diary entries on a blog or recording and uploading audio diaries. Participants can also use various software programs to map their social networks, draw diagrams of their workspaces, or create photo collages as part of data collection. It is important for researchers to understand the benefits and drawbacks of in-person versus distance modes of engagement so data collected from participants can be the best that it can be. Where budgets or other logistical details do not allow for in-person data collection, technology can provide the next best approach for many qualitative projects, however, there are a number of questions to ask when deciding to use technology in place of an in-person technique:

- Will the participant be comfortable using the technology?
- Does the participant have the appropriate hardware, software, Internet connection, and so on, needed for data collection?
- Can the research team provide appropriate technology support for participants?

- What privacy, copyright, or other issues could arise due to the use of technology?
- What research ethics issues might arise due to the use of technology?
- What are the budgetary, logistical, and other considerations of technology-based data collection compared to in-person approaches?

More questions? See #21, #71, and #86.

There Are Many Interviews and Other Potential Sources of Data Online, Including People's Quotes Posted to Social Media and Websites. Can I Use These in My Qualitative Study?

There are many rich sources of data online, and qualitative researchers have been making good use of these sources. Interviews with politicians appear on news websites, teenagers upload personal video diaries to YouTube, and restaurant patrons post their favorite food pictures and commentary on social media. All of these sources offer rich data that may be analyzed using qualitative approaches. Existing datasets like these can provide easy, cost-effective access to hundreds of hours (or pages) of content, often from individuals around the world and representing diverse backgrounds. These sources may be used alone, or they may complement original data collection conducted by the researcher as part of a larger study.

However these datasets are used, the need for ethics review is a key consideration for all researchers. It is important to understand the nature and origin of the dataset and to examine its source in the context of the ethics guidelines that govern the researcher's work. In many cases, these data will not require ethics review; where materials are in the public domain, for example, they can be accessed and analyzed in ways similar to the way researchers would use materials in a public archive or when published in the newspaper. Where data are housed within a private website, or where a social media tool requires membership to view content, ethics review may be required prior to data collection and analysis. It is important for researchers to understand the nature of the dataset and seek advice from relevant ethics review boards, as needed.

More questions? See #17, #39, and #70.

I See That Some Qualitative Studies Use Participant-Generated Photographs, Drawings, and Other Arts-Based Approaches. When Is It Appropriate to Use These Kinds of Methods for Gathering Data?

Many qualitative researchers engage participants in arts-based activities during data collection. Generally, these approaches fall into two main categories: participant-response activities and participant-generation activities. Participant-response activities involve the use of various media (such as videos, photographs, excerpts of text) to engage participants in discussion. A focus group may be shown an advertisement for a new product and asked to comment on the content and aesthetics of the ad. An interviewee may be asked to read an online newspaper article and comment on the layout and navigation of the news website. Seniors may be asked to look at photos from their childhood to discuss what life was like when they were growing up. The documents themselves may form part of the dataset (e.g., where a researcher conducts a content analysis of photographs discussed during an interview). However, the focus of the activity is on the participant's response to the media at hand.

Participant-generated, arts-based activities are also used to enhance a range of qualitative methods. Young children, for example, may be asked to draw a picture that represents their family life as part of an interview process. Teens may be asked to take photographs to discuss safety issues in their school environments. A group of seniors living in a retirement community may draw maps of their social networks. In these cases, the participant-generated documents are a primary focus for the analysis. Participants may provide commentary on the meaning or importance of the image, but the researcher is also interested in analyzing the content of the created object.

Participant-response and participant-generated, arts-based approaches are used to

- Put participants at ease by providing a focus for the discussion;
- Provide concrete examples to participants to prompt brainstorming activities;
- Break up the monotony of another lengthy method (e.g., a long interview);
- Personalize the activity by providing participants the opportunity to share or create personal photographs, diaries, and other artifacts; and
- Engage with particular populations in ways that best suit their stage of development or personal circumstances.

More questions? See #11, #39, and #53.

I Have a Lot of Data—Dozens of Digital Data Files, Hundreds of Pages of Printed Transcripts, and Hours of Video-Recordings. How Can I Manage All of This Material?

One of the great benefits of qualitative research is that each method can generate dozens of data files, hundreds of pages of documents, and hours of recordings for future analysis. The downside is that a researcher must establish an approach to data management that will allow for long-term access and use, without becoming overwhelmed. There are a number of resources now for research data management and many support staff (such as librarians) that can help researchers to develop appropriate practices. The following are some key points to consider when managing the vast amount of data generated in qualitative projects:

- Make backup copies of everything;
- Store materials securely, with backup copies in another secure (physical or virtual) location;
- Budget for the purchase of back-up materials (such as external hard drives, cloud storage);
- Create a system of folders and file names for managing digital and print resources before you gather your data;
- Train research team members in the use of your folder and file name scheme so that shared materials are easily located;
- Choose established software packages for transcription and analysis, preferably with technical support, to allow for long-term storage (i.e., where software updates will be included); and
- Apply appropriate ethical practices in managing data files and ensure that these are outlined in ethics applications.

More questions? See #12, #24, and #86.

How Do I Know When I've Reached Saturation of Themes in My Data?

Saturation of themes occurs at the point that additional data do not lead to any new emergent themes. As new data are analyzed they will contribute to the researcher's understanding and interpretation of the phenomenon under study. The analysis process is iterative so as new themes emerge, the data that have already been analyzed are reexamined to see if (and how) the new themes may alter the interpretation. When new data repeat themes that are already identified in the analysis, these new data provide confirming evidence of the identified themes. If new data do not contribute new themes or patterns in the analysis process, a researcher may determine that saturation of themes has been reached. When new themes emerge in a dataset, with few examples noted in data collected previously, additional participants might need to be recruited to examine the new themes in detail. In this way, saturation can also guide the theoretical sampling process to ensure that sufficient evidence is gathered to support the various emergent themes.

Although the stage at which saturation is reached will vary with each project and will depend on the nature and complexity of the data being gathered, some general guidelines have been developed to guide the sampling process to fit with thematic saturation. In interview methods, for example, researchers typically expect to see saturation of themes once 15 to 18 interviews have been conducted. Researchers will generally aim to collect data from additional participants to provide confirming evidence, so they may sample more than 20 or 25 participants in a qualitative study. However, this number will provide saturation for thematic analysis across the full dataset. If a researcher plans to make comparisons within the dataset (such as comparing men's attitudes to women's, or comparing youth, adult, and seniors' perceptions to one another), sampling to saturation within each of those groups is necessary. This can increase the size of the study significantly.

More questions? See #36, #43, and #82.

My Colleague Says That There Are Many "Lost Opportunities" in His Dataset. What Does That Mean?

When qualitative researchers listen to recordings, review transcripts, watch video recordings, or reflect on their data collection processes, they will often identify areas where they wished they had gathered more data. In listening to a focus group interview, for example, a participant may raise an issue that was not then discussed; the topic may have gotten lost in the conversation, with many people talking at once, and never be revisited by the group. Similarly, when researchers review a video recording of observational data, they may see an activity happening at the edge of the screen but without enough detail to allow for thorough analysis. These types of experiences are often referred to as "lost opportunities" because they represent possible opportunities for additional or deeper analysis that were lost in the data collection process. If researchers have planned to do follow-up interviews, for example, they may be able to "recover" the lost data. Or, they may be able to adjust the data collection process to be sure to capture similar data from that point forward. In many cases, however, these lost data simply serve as reminders that researchers are human and cannot capture everything, no matter how thorough or well-executed the project design. As long as the lost opportunities are rare and do not affect the researcher's ability to provide sufficient evidence for the findings presented, these instances do not adversely affect the quality of the project. However, these lost opportunities may also become areas for future research.

More questions? See #12, #61, and #90.

I'm Trying to Select the Best Site for Conducting Individual Interviews, So How Do I Choose?

There are many elements to consider in selecting the ideal location for a one-on-one interview with a participant. In some cases, a researcher asks participants to choose, believing that this will allow them to feel more at ease with the process. However, if a participant selects a noisy or busy location, for example, the researcher may not be able to gather data under optimal conditions. Whether the researcher selects the site, or if she or he simply educates participants about the type of location to choose, the following details are preferable for interviews:

- **Quiet.** The interviewing process is intense, requiring both the researcher and the participant to engage with and reflect on the topics being discussed. A quiet environment, free from other distractions, is important. Interviewing participants in their homes, for example, may mean that children, pets, couriers, telephones, or other distractions may arise during the interview. Conducting an interview in a local coffee shop may mean that other regular customers may drop by the table and interrupt the flow of the discussion. Ensuring that the location is quiet and free from distractions is vital to success.
- **Private.** Participants need to feel free to discuss topics without any worry of being overheard by others. This is important for topics that deal with sensitive issues, or where a participant has concerns about being identified. Ensuring that a space is private and will provide the confidentiality needed for frank and open discussions is very important.
- **Comfortable.** The physical space for the interview needs to be comfortable for both the participant and the researcher. Temperature, lighting, furnishings, and other details are important to consider in selecting a space. If an interview is expected to last several hours, the comfort of the space will be particularly important for both parties.

- **Appropriate for interviewing activities (if any).** Many interviews include a range of activities, such as searching on a computer, reviewing documents, or drawing pictures, in addition to talking with participants. Ensuring that the space has the appropriate table space, equipment, or other requirements for tasks to be conducted during the interview is a key requirement. In these cases, the researcher may wish to select the space so that the location can be properly set up, in advance of each interview.
- **Appropriate for technology use (if any).** If a researcher is using a recording device, space for a tripod or access to a power plug may be an important factor in the location selected for the interview. In these cases, the researcher may need to select the location, in order to ensure it will be appropriate for the data collection technology that will be used.

More questions? See #16, #65, and #69.

PART 8

CONDUCTING QUALITATIVE ANALYSIS

Do I Have to Wait Until My Data Collection Is Done Before I Can Start Analyzing My Data?

In qualitative research, data analysis begins with the start of data collection. Although much of the data analysis (and writing) will be done once all of the data are gathered, researchers typically begin to think about, reflect on, and explore the nature of the findings alongside data collection. For this reason, qualitative projects are described as inductive and emergent in their design, with data analysis starting from the moment that the first pieces of data are gathered. The researcher begins to interpret what is seen in the data immediately and may adjust the data collection process to suit the initial findings that emerge. For example, when participants raise experiences that researchers had not anticipated, it is common to alter the interview questions with subsequent participants to ensure that data about these new experiences will be captured. The process involves active engagement and analytical thinking and reflection to ensure that relevant data are gathered to address the project's research questions. This initial thinking and reflection is all part of an analytic process, as the researcher is already beginning to make sense of the data, even at the early stages of data collection. Although the bulk of analysis work may happen once all data are gathered, researchers will make field notes and start to write down their initial analytic impressions to inform the later, in-depth analysis work that they will do.

When large teams are involved in a project, especially where assistants or others conduct data collection, it is important to hold regular analytic debriefing sessions during data collection. This will ensure that initial analyses inform changes in data collection implementation (as needed). These sessions will also ensure that the primary investigators are immersed in the dataset from an early stage, so they can begin the process of analysis with a clear sense of the dataset and where the initial findings are starting to lead.

More questions? See #31, #83, and #89.

My Supervisor Says I Should Use an Interpretive Lens for My Analysis—What Does This Mean?

The idea of having an "interpretive lens" is one that many researchers discuss when talking about their analysis practices. In inductive, emergent designs, theorizing about and interpreting the data begins during data collection and continues through analysis. The data drive the analysis process so that the researcher is able to engage with various theoretical lenses as part of this process. At times, a researcher develops a unique theory about the phenomenon under examination. Or, a researcher may choose to turn a particular "interpretive lens" on the data to guide the analysis process. A feminist lens, for example, may be used where the thematic analysis and coding process contribute to feminist theory. Various elements emerging in an observational dataset, for example, might point to gender differences in how students are treated in the classroom. The researcher may decide to delve deeply into an analysis of those portions of the dataset where gendered experiences are evident and use a particular feminist theory (or set of theories) to inform the analysis process.

The concept of a "lens" for analysis speaks to the process of isolating particular elements of the dataset as part of interpretive analysis. Just as a camera lens frames a particular action and pushes other details to the edges of the frame, an interpretive lens focuses the analysis on particular issues, activities, or experiences evident in the dataset. Typically, the lens will first be drawn by the boundaries set out by the research questions; however, it will also be informed by the theory that is used to inform the researcher's analysis. Using feminist standpoint theory as a lens, for example, will lead to a very different interpretation of the data than the use of feminist postmodern theory. As the process of analysis proceeds and themes emerge, additional theoretical approaches may be applied to the dataset to enhance the researcher's interpretation of the data.

More questions? See #6, #32, and #33.

What Is the Process for "Coding" My Dataset? Can I Borrow Someone Else's Codebook to Get Me Started?

The process of coding data is unique for each project, where the development of a codebook is a key part of the work that is needed for a full analysis. A codebook is a document that outlines the various codes assigned to portions of the data, including how those codes are defined and applied in the context of the research questions. Coding is influenced by the project design, its methodology and the methods used, as well as the overarching research problem addressed in the study. However, coding is also heavily influenced by the researcher's own background, previous experiences, and epistemological worldview. Coding may also be influenced by the end goal of the analysis and writing process. For example, although one publication arising from the data may be quite descriptive in nature, other publications may be highly theoretical; the coding process and terms used for these different analysis outcomes will also vary.

Coding typically involves a deep reading of the dataset to address the research questions being explored. Analysis and interpretation of the data leads to the development of thematic codes, or terms that represent the underlying concepts that are prevalent in the data. Often, researchers will focus their writing on a few key conceptual themes (depending on the scale and purpose of the document they are writing), leaving other thematic codes for future, in-depth analysis. Determining which coded themes are of primary importance (and which are secondary, tertiary, etc.) will be guided by the research questions, methodology, and theoretical framework for the study. Coding practices may vary with each researcher's interpretation of the data due to the influence of epistemological worldview and personal context; however, rigorous data collection and analysis practices will ensure that evidence drawn from the dataset supports the analytic interpretations.

For these reasons, "borrowing" someone else's codebook is not a solution for a researcher who is trying to code his or her own data. A codebook cannot be applied to other, unrelated datasets, even though a researcher may use similar codes in future projects. However, reviewing other researchers' codebooks can provide useful models from which to develop a new codebook, particularly for novice scholars. Similarly, engaging co-investigators, research assistants, or study participants in the coding process can help to guide the analysis process. Although some codes may be relatively easy to identify and apply to the dataset (such as marking an interview with a code for "internet use" whenever a participant mentions engaging in that activity), other concepts (such as identifying feelings of "fear" or "joy") may be more difficult to code. Involving other people in the process of thematic analysis can aid the coding process. However, researchers must be careful to ensure that such involvement is covered in their initial ethics application so that they can share data with others as part of this process.

More questions? See #77, #79, and #83.

What Is the Difference Between "Themes," "Codes," and "Categories"?

Qualitative researchers use a mix of terms to describe the analysis processes in which they engage. These terms will vary depending on the methodology used in the particular study, so researchers need to review and define key concepts within the context of the specific research design they have chosen. However, there are some common ways to think about the analytic concepts that emerge during qualitative analysis. Often called "emergent themes," these concepts are the core findings related to the patterns and issues that arise from inductive analysis of qualitative data. In any single dataset, several major and minor themes will emerge related to the research questions examined in the study. Codes are labels that are assigned to those themes as they emerge. Coding terms are selected carefully, in order to ensure that the context informing the thematic concept is represented appropriately. Categories are groups of codes used to highlight the complexities of themes, particularly the ways that they fit—or do not fit—together in the analysis. The following table provides an example of how themes might be represented in a coding and categorization scheme:

Research Problem:
How do young children engage with technology as part of early literacy learning?

Table 80.1. Comparing Themes, Codes and Categories

Theme = Importance of social interaction during technology use	Codes	Categories
Codes re: "Who" they interact with	Parents, siblings, grandparents, etc.	Family
	Other children, parents of other children, etc.	Friends
	Teachers, librarians, etc.	Instructors
Codes re: "How" they interact	Singing, laughing, etc.	Responding to technology
	Asking questions, talking to others, etc.	Learning about technology

In this example, the theme addressing the "importance of social interaction during technology use" has a number of codes and categories that may explore elements of the theme. The table presents just two of these codes (related to the people with whom the children interact and how the children interact with those people). The categories are used to group similar codes to demonstrate the various types of people and the different ways children interact with those people. It is important to note that this example is not exhaustive; there may be many other codes assigned to the theme, depending on the scope of the investigation. Similarly, there will be various other themes that emerge from the dataset. Researchers make conscious decisions at all stages of the analysis in identifying and labeling the theme and in noting the codes and categories that address elements of each theme.

More questions? See #31, #77, and #78.

Does the Person Who Gathered the Data Have to Be the Person Who Codes and Analyzes Those Data?

Ideally in qualitative research, the person who gathers the data is the same person who codes and analyzes those data. In part, this is because the nature of the process means that analysis is happening alongside data collection, so gathering and analysis are not two separate processes entirely. Although the bulk of data analysis and coding will happen after data collection is complete, this is not always the case; the process depends on the methodology used, as well as practical logistics. For example, in an ethnographic study where a researcher is embedded in a particular research site for many months and is gathering data in an unstructured way, that person will be collecting, analyzing, and coding data as the study proceeds. However, in a grounded theory study with a series of single-session, semistructured interviews, a research assistant may conduct the interviews and the principal researcher may be involved at the analytical stage. There are many different combinations of roles and tasks that are taken on in qualitative projects.

Researchers must be involved in all phases of the work, even if the degree of involvement varies across stages of the project. As data collection is informed by the research design (including the research questions to be addressed in the study), the principal researcher must monitor and guide data collection completed by other people. Regular debriefing sessions to modify interview guides, for example, are important for success. During these sessions, initial analysis will also be conducted, so the researcher can begin to see how the findings may emerge. Similarly, in the later phases of analysis, a researcher may ask another person to engage deeply in the process; this can be particularly useful if that person was involved in data collection, as she or he would already have a sense of the dataset and initial analysis themes. As long as researchers understand that data collection and analysis cannot be fully "offloaded" to another person, they can certainly engage others in these processes. If done well, the other people serve as "surrogates" for the researcher, where they can understand the project's goals and make wise choices in the moment of data collection or analysis, which will serve those goals.

More questions? See #31, #77, and #83.

I've Heard Data Analysis Described as an Iterative Process of Coding. What Does That Mean?

Qualitative data analysis is described as "iterative" because the process cycles back on itself as patterns and themes emerge from the data. When a researcher identifies a new theme after analyzing 10 interview transcripts, for example, that new theme may raise questions about the data that have already been analyzed. To ensure all relevant data are coded for that new theme, the researcher needs to go back and review the first few transcripts again, to see how (or if) the new analytical theme alters the interpretation of the data. This process will happen several times during the course of analysis, until the researcher reaches a full saturation of themes represented in the dataset.

As new sources of data are added (through triangulation of methods, participants, or settings, for example), further iteration of analysis may be needed to explore the themes fully. Data collection may also be part of this iterative analysis process; for example, where follow-up interviews are held with participants, initial analysis of the first sets of interviews may change based on the results of the follow-up interviews. As new data are gathered, these lead to new findings; as new findings emerge, these lead to new analyses of the existing dataset. The process continues to cycle across all of the data gathered, from all sources, until the analytical process is complete.

More questions? See #39, #78, and #90.

How Can I Use a Team to Code Data?

The process of data analysis, including coding of data, begins with the initial stages of data collection. Researchers start to think about the patterns they are seeing in the data and what those patterns might mean, which can then affect how data are gathered as the project moves ahead. In a solo project, the researcher is at the center of all of these stages—that is, gathering the data, thinking about meaning, identifying codes for analysis, and writing up the results. However, when other people are involved in the project (whether hired staff, students, or co-investigators), the "team" becomes integral to the data analysis process. Every person on the team will have ideas about the data being gathered, will start to identify patterns and themes, and will have opinions on how best to code data and frame the analysis and writing.

Most researchers use this type of "group think" to their advantage, by encouraging team members to "own" the dataset, conceptually, and contribute to the group's thinking about the data in productive ways. However, even when this type of open dialogue and theorizing is used among the team members, just one person may complete the formal act of coding the full dataset. Often, this is done for pragmatic reasons. Using a software package for analysis, for example, may require that one individual input codes into the system, which can then be viewed by the rest of the team later on. Similarly, research team members with particular expertise may code the data for themes related to their particular area; this approach is quite common in interdisciplinary teams, where key themes are best identified (and coded) by the individual working in a particular topic area.

Some researchers, however, choose to engage the full team in the theorizing process. A series of team meetings to identify and code common patterns and themes may be held, where individuals use whiteboards, flipcharts, data projectors, and other collaborative tools to conduct a group analysis of the dataset. This approach can be useful, particularly to see the data through various people's perspectives and to identify the most salient themes related to various areas of expertise. However, the success of such an approach often relies on people being co-located to conduct the work.

Group sessions with some (or all) individuals at a distance from one another are very difficult to coordinate and may not be as effective as in-person group analysis. For this reason, some research teams plan retreats as part of the main analytical work (i.e., once all data are gathered) to facilitate group interaction.

More questions? See #11, #31, and #77.

Do Qualitative Researchers Count Things in Their Data, or Is This Only Done in Quantitative Research?

Qualitative researchers do count things when conducting data analysis. They may count how often participants use a particular word to describe themselves, or they may count the number of people who use a particular technology. Researchers may choose to present these descriptive counts in tables or pie graphs in their research reports to provide the reader with a visual representation of these quantitative data. However, counting instances of a thing is not the primary goal of qualitative research design. A researcher conducting a discourse analysis of a policy document, for example, may want to count the number of times that particular words appear. If a document describes homeless youth as "at risk" on a regular basis, throughout the document, the researcher may want to point to the frequency of use of the term to point to the power of language in shaping a reader's understanding of the issue. In this way, the decision to conduct a frequency count is used to complement a deep analysis of the text; although the researcher may present these data in tables or using word clouds to illustrate the results, these representations are typically few in number and secondary to the textual presentation of quoted excerpts from the text.

Here is an example of a word cloud, created using the paragraph that you have just read. The most frequent words in the text ("researcher," "document," and "count") appear larger in the image than the words that only appear once (such as "power").

Figure 84.1 Example of a Word Cloud

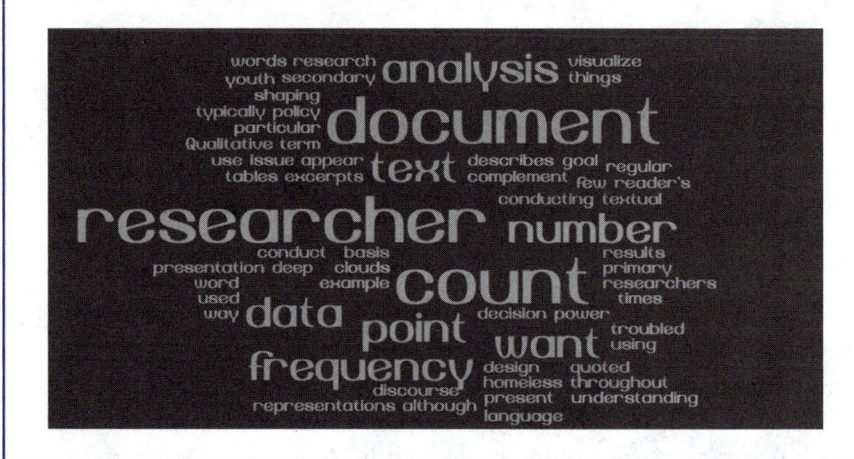

More questions? See #8, #91, and #95.

Will Using a Qualitative Data Analysis Software Package Improve the Quality of My Results?

Using qualitative data analysis software packages will not necessarily improve the quality of the study's results. Although these packages provide many tools and features that can enhance the data analysis process (from visualization techniques to quick data retrieval), the quality of the results relies on the care taken by the researcher in doing the intellectual work of data analysis. Ensuring that all data are coded, that terms and concepts are used consistently, and that all data sources are analyzed together as part of the triangulation process are just some of the considerations that need to be made.

Unfortunately, referring to these tools as "data analysis" software packages can be misleading, as the program cannot replace the researcher's own thinking and analysis process. Software packages (such as NVivo, Atlas.ti, MaxQDA, and others) provide researchers with a number of analytic tools that can aid the data coding and analysis process. Being able to retrieve coded sections of a transcript quickly, or to visualize how various codes align across multiple participant files, is very helpful in the analysis process. However, these tools might more accurately be called "data management" tools, as their primary benefit to researchers is that they offer many ways to manage, label, and review data files in the analysis process.

Many qualitative researchers choose to analyze their data without using specialized software programs, relying instead on software designed for other purposes (such as using the comments feature in Word to code sections of a transcript). As part of the analysis and writing process, researchers may also use whiteboards to map data relationships, they may use colored pens to mark themes on print transcripts, or they may categorize photographs in a dataset using sticky notes. Whatever tool is used, the quality of the results relies on the researcher using a thorough and systematic approach to analysis.

More questions? See #39, #81, and #86.

What Is the Best Software Package to Use for Qualitative Data Analysis?

Many qualitative researchers use software packages to manage qualitative data. There are many fee-based packages on the market (such as NVivo, Atlas.ti, and MaxQDA), available for single use, multiuser licenses and site licenses for large organizations. Most have educational rates for students and for individuals working at universities or other educational institutions. The features vary for each package; researchers need to investigate which one will best suit their needs for a particular project, depending on the types of data gathered and in what formats.

It is important to note that referring to these software packages as "qualitative data analysis" packages is not quite accurate. Although the software will help researchers to manage data and can aid data analysis, especially across large datasets, the software cannot do the intellectual work of thematic analysis and coding. Researchers must analyze their data and code within the system. Once the codes are entered, data can be retrieved quickly, results can be visualized using various tools designed for theorizing, and codes can be examined alongside other codes, offering unique approaches to analysis.

In many cases, existing desktop software may be all that is needed for data analysis. Many researchers code transcripts in Word, illustrate theoretical relationships using PowerPoint, and create content analysis schema in Excel. Many software tools that researchers use every day can be adapted for data analysis, which is particularly useful when dealing with small datasets or when specialized software is too costly. Many researchers also work with data in print form, flagging codes using multicolored highlighters, sticky notes, and whiteboards.

When making the decision to purchase qualitative analysis software, researchers need to ask the following questions:

1. Is specialized software necessary given the goals of this project?

2. Do I have existing tools (software or print sources) that can be used instead?

3. What data formats can I use with this software?

4. What training will be needed to use the package? Does this increase costs?

5. Can every member of the research team access the software? Does this increase costs?

6. When does the license expire? Am I required to renew the fee to access my data?

7. Does my institution support this software (e.g., site license; technical support)?

More questions? See #73, #81, and #85.

Does It Matter if Someone Else Interprets My Results in a Different Way?

As qualitative research design is embedded in a constructionist view of reality, it is expected that different people will interpret the data in different ways. The researcher presents "an" interpretation of the data, which is supported by the evidence and grounded in existing disciplinary knowledge, rather than "the" interpretation of the data. This does not mean that the interpretation is not robust or appropriate. Rather, it speaks to the influence of context, culture, history, and worldview on the interpretive analytical process. Researchers approaching a project's design with different contexts, cultures, histories, and worldviews will design projects in different ways. If the evidence gathered can support multiple interpretations of the data, those interpretations are sound.

Often, qualitative researchers will account for potential multiple interpretations when writing about the results of the study. Presenting anomalous data as part of a negative case analysis, for example, is one way to point to the fact that thematic analysis is not meant to present the "final" story about participants' experiences. Similarly, researchers may note where specific data conflict with established knowledge about a particular issue, and make the point that future data collection and analysis may be warranted to understand that issue in more depth.

More questions? See #5, #8, and #22.

I Have Anomalous Data. Is This a Problem?

Examining anomalous data is one of the ways that qualitative analysis presents rich, deep findings that illuminate many sides of an issue. Although the goal in qualitative analysis generally is to explore themes and patterns that are common to participants or data collection sites, examining data that do not "fit" with the common trends is another important part of the analytical process. This process is also called negative case analysis, which refers to the process of looking at the data points that go in a different direction from the primary theme.

For example, a study of seniors' Internet use may find that a common theme emerging from the dataset is an anxiety about computer use; participants may express a range of negative emotions as they talk about their lack of comfort with technology, their fear of making a mistake, or their lack of confidence in going online. However, there may be one participant who is extremely comfortable with the technology. That senior may teach others to use the Internet, she may talk about the joy she feels at being able to engage with her family online, and she may talk about how confident and empowered she feels using technology. This senior's experience is a negative case, or one that goes against the majority perspective in the dataset. Rather than ignoring the finding, or only briefly noting that such a case exists, a qualitative researcher will spend a great deal of time analyzing the experience of this one individual. If the interview with this senior happens late in data collection, where it is clear that this is a negative case, the researcher may also alter the interview guide to delve into her experience in more detail.

It may be helpful to think about the adage "the exception that proves the rule" when considering the role of anomalous data in the qualitative analysis process. The presence of a single, anomalous case demonstrates just how embedded the others' perspectives are within the population. However, the single case also demonstrates that change is possible, that not all people need to feel negative emotions in the same situation, and that key informants could be used (when applying the research results in practice) to help others change their perspectives. By understanding the nuances of the anomalous case, including why the person feels empowered, how they became comfortable with the Internet, or what advice they would have for seniors who feel anxiety when using technology, the discussion of findings related to the "anxiety" theme can be enhanced and enriched.

More questions? See #74, #90, and #91.

I've Heard That I Need to Immerse Myself in the Data During Analysis, but I Have a Full-Time Job. How Much Time Do I Need to Devote to This Process?

Many qualitative research tasks require sustained periods of attention to do justice to the work. Academics, clinicians, and other qualitative researchers are often conducting research activities while balancing teaching, administrative, clinical, or other duties. These various tasks create a heavy cognitive load for the researcher, who must balance a busy time schedule, as well as the intellectual demands of qualitative analysis work. Even when researchers are working on their projects on a full-time basis (such as some doctoral students or contract researchers), personal commitments can often be challenging to manage around intense periods of qualitative data collection and analysis. Immersing oneself in the data is vital to ensure that the data are fully analyzed, particularly as the process is iterative and inductive, requiring intense intellectual work to identify patterns and themes. Where data are drawn from various sources, cross-comparisons across datasets will also require periods of deep engagement with the material. The nature of qualitative research requires that researchers become immersed in their datasets at the analysis stage, even where others have been involved in data collection, transcription, or project planning. The analysis process begins with the project design and with initial data collection; however, the majority of the analysis work occurs once the data are gathered, transcribed, and ready for deep intellectual thematizing.

Although many researchers are able to work particular tasks (such as transcription) around other day-to-day commitments, most find that qualitative analysis is one activity that requires sustained periods of uninterrupted time for successful completion. Once data are collected, transcribed, downloaded, or otherwise managed, the data analysis process can take weeks or months to complete. An important first step is to break the analysis process into pieces so that the analysis process can be completed while attending to other tasks. For example, analyzing data from interviews, separately from other data sources, may be possible so that the analysis work can be scheduled over separate blocks of time. Several days of uninterrupted time are needed to dig into the data and begin the process of thematic coding and analysis. The amount of time will vary, project to project, and depend on the researcher's previous experience with analysis; however, most people find that they need more time than they might think. It is quite common for researchers to take several months to analyze data, planning for a few days each week to devote to this work. When working full-time, researchers may need to plan analysis time during their weekend hours or consider taking vacation days to get through large blocks of work.

More questions? See #13, #14, and #81.

My Analysis Seems to Raise More Questions Than Answers, So What Do I Do About This?

One of the interesting outcomes of all research is that the process itself is cyclical; although researchers design projects to fill knowledge gaps in their fields, they rarely find "the answer" to their question. Typically, qualitative researchers will learn a great deal in their projects, including what there is still to be learned! Research often raises more questions, particularly in projects that use inductive, emergent designs. Until a researcher is in the field, he or she cannot know what the participants' experiences of a phenomenon will be. Once in the field, the researcher gathers data to understand the phenomenon; however, there will be many elements of that understanding that will need to become part of a new research project. As a part of the analysis and writing process, qualitative researchers will document those areas that require additional research. They publish what they can, based on the evidence gathered, and then start to design the next study, which will provide deeper—or different—insights into the research topic. This process is not unique to qualitative research; however, it can feel overwhelming to new researchers, who see that the data in hand are very rich, yet may raise more questions for the future. This is a very positive outcome of qualitative research; when new findings point to areas requiring further investigation, researchers can begin to see their program of research unfolding. A full program of research can take several years, even becoming a life's work, which can sustain the qualitative researcher over the path of his or her career.

More questions? See #15, #74, and #96.

PART 9

WRITING QUALITATIVE RESEARCH

How Do I Present My Findings So That They Reflect Both My Analysis and the Participants' Voices?

There is a craft to writing qualitative results so that they balance the researcher's voice with that of the participants and also analyze the data in the context of the published literature. In quantitative studies, the "results" (i.e., the data or evidence) of a study are separated, typically, from the "discussion" of the meaning of those results, followed by the "conclusions." In qualitative writing, the data and their meanings are integrated into what is often labeled "findings and discussion," followed by a separate "conclusions" section. It is in this "findings and discussion" section that the primary analysis, including participants' voices, is presented.

Qualitative researchers need to balance three "voices" in their writing about the research results: the data (participants' voices), the interpretation of data (researcher's voice), and the published literature (disciplinary voice). Generally, the writing will begin with the researcher's voice, to establish the interpretive voice at an early stage in the writing and to make claims about the themes uncovered during analysis. However, in writing the interpretive statements, the researcher consciously weaves the participants' voices into the text so that their perspectives appear alongside the researcher's voice. The researcher may use direct quotes as headings in the text as well, to frame the various themes around the participants' voices. Finally, in guiding the analysis of the data, the researcher will draw on the published literature to ground the findings in the disciplinary evidence and demonstrate how the data confirm or contrast with the existing body of knowledge.

An excerpt of text in the findings section of a journal article, might look like this:

> *The seniors interviewed in this study spoke at length about their fears and anxieties in using technology, particularly when others were watching the activity. These fears manifested*

themselves in both cognitive and physical ways, which could be quite debilitating for these seniors. John, for example, described his physical responses, noting, "My chest tightens, I begin to sweat.... It's just so overwhelming." Mary expressed concerns about her own emotional safety, saying, "I don't want to appear stupid, or like I don't know what I'm doing." For these seniors, the use of technology was not a simple or straightforward task, requiring only knowledge of how the computer worked or what websites to search online. Rather, there were a number of mental and physical blocks that needed to be overcome to be able to use technology effectively. This finding is consistent with the published literature, which explores... [And the narrative continues here, drawing the literature into the analysis framework.]

Here, the narrative begins with the researcher's voice, with the participants' experiences drawn in to provide evidence to support the claims being made. The literature will then flow into the discussion to highlight where this experience sits within the broader research literature in the discipline. Throughout the complete section, the researcher will draw in a range of different participants to make the case, including a discussion of any anomalous data. Published literature that supports, or conflicts with, the interpretation will be discussed as well. In the end, the narrative will present the interpretation, the evidence to support that interpretation, and draw on the published literature so that the reader can see how the results of the study contribute to knowledge.

More questions? See #9, #10, and #93.

I've Assigned My Participants Numbers (to Keep Them Anonymous in the Writing) but Now My Supervisor Says I Should Give Them Pseudonyms Instead. Which Approach Is Best?

Researchers use various approaches to anonymize participants when writing up the results of their research. In some cases, participants are assigned numbers (such as "Interviewee #14") or they are represented by generic demographic details designed to shield their identity (such as "15-year-old boy participant"). Some researchers even create intricate coding systems to reflect data collection details pertinent to the dataset, which help them to organize their files; for example, a participant might be coded as "MI3/2" as a short-form for "Male Interviewee #3/2nd interview."

However, in most qualitative studies, researchers select pseudonyms to represent their participants' real names. The use of personal names helps to humanize the participants so that the reader can see the person behind the data being presented. In many cases, researchers will choose a personal first name (such as "Joe" or "Suzie"); in others, they may use a more formal name that includes detail about the participant's role or title (such as "Professor Jones" or "Reverend Martin"). Some researchers also let participants choose their own pseudonym, whether from a list of preselected names or a name created by the participant at the time the data are collected.

The use of pseudonyms (rather than alpha-numeric codes) also aids the narrative writing style commonly used in qualitative studies. Being able to talk about a participant's personal narrative is made easier when the individual can be mentioned by name, particularly when provided alongside personal details about the participant's situation. For example, a researcher might write the following statement as a prelude to a relevant quote:

"Brian, a 35-year-old father of two young children, had this to say about the importance of parent support groups. . . ."

There are a number of key points to keep in mind when assigning participants' pseudonyms:

1. It is important that each pseudonym be unique, so that the reader can distinguish data drawn from each participant easily and clearly. Researchers may need to assign unique names across several data-sets to aid comparative analysis in future writing.

2. Consideration should be given to cultural, social, or other contexts relevant to the study, which may affect pseudonym selection. For example, using women's and men's names to represent female and male participants (respectively) may be the best choice when gender is an important element in analysis; in other cases, selecting a gender-neutral name (such as "Pat") may be the best choice.

3. The use of pseudonyms should be directly noted in the writing of the publication, to alert the reader to the fact that participants' real names have been removed. Often, this is done in a footnote at the first mention of a pseudonym and may include details about how the pseudonyms were chosen.

More questions? See #9, #16, and #93.

My Supervisor Says I Should "Give Voice" to My Research Participants in My Writing—What Does That Mean?

Qualitative research is designed to examine individuals' perceptions and experiences of the world around them. Researchers interpret these findings in the analysis process, but the goal is to ensure that the project reflects the participants' views in the writing of the project results. For this reason, researchers often talk about "giving voice" to the participants as a way to keep these individuals at the forefront of the writing process, to ensure that their perspectives are heard in the project reports. For example, research publications will typically include lengthy quotes to illustrate key findings. Similarly, the writing style will push the participants to the forefront, rather than privileging the researcher's voice. Researchers must balance the need to present their interpretations of the data (the "researcher voice") with evidence drawn from the dataset (the "participant voice"). Researchers may use the following techniques to give voice to participants:

- Providing lengthy quotes drawn from the dataset to illustrate interpretations of the evidence, rather than relying on paraphrasing or short quotes alone;
- Using participants' terminology to describe situations and experiences, rather than imposing the researcher's own language;
- Including photographs, artwork, and other original sources provided by participants during data collection, alongside quoted statements; and
- Reviewing written excerpts with participants (i.e., member checking) to ensure that the researcher's representation of the data best reflects the participants' experiences.

It is also important to note that the process of "giving voice" does not simply happen at the end of the project during the writing process.

The research design itself must ensure that participants are involved and able to have their voices heard in the project. For example, if a project is designed to study patients' experiences of the emergency room, it is not enough to only talk to the doctors and nurses involved. Doing so would provide data on health care practitioners' perceptions of the patients' experience—but the patients themselves would be silenced in the study. Although practitioners' perspectives are valuable in this context (and would be a useful way to triangulate the study), only patients themselves can give voice to their experiences. When designing a study, researchers may use the following techniques to ensure that participants' voices are heard:

- Engaging with key stakeholders (e.g., a community group) at the design phase to ensure that the project's goals address participants' experiences, from their perspective;
- Using triangulation of participant groups so that a range of stakeholders may reflect on the phenomenon being studied;
- Asking participants to provide material for analysis (e.g., photographs, sample texts), rather than relying solely on researcher-developed texts and prompts; and
- Capturing data in a permanent, textual form (e.g., audio recordings, participant-written diaries) to ensure that participants' reflections are transcribed, verbatim, in project reports.

More questions? See #39, #88, and #91.

I Have Some Pictures, Audio Recordings, and Other Multimedia Data, So How Can I Include These in Publications?

Aside from the content of multimedia materials (which can be analyzed thematically by the researcher), photographs, audio files, video recordings, artwork, and other types of materials can also be used to enhance traditional writing and dissemination of qualitative results. During conference presentations, workshops with community partners, or seminars to industry and government, visual representations of data (such as charts, graphs, and images) can be used to capture the attention and imagination of the audience and allow people to engage deeply with the content being presented. Where a quote from a participant suffering a chronic illness can provide a powerful example of what it means to live with that disease, an audio excerpt of that same quote, or a photograph of the person connected to many wires and tubes in their hospital bed, can heighten the impact of the content. Although a multimedia presentation may require more advanced planning (e.g., to ensure that audio can be streamed in the room or that data files will play on various devices), the benefits can far outweigh the additional time and effort needed to create this type of presentation.

It may be possible to use some types of media in written research publications as well, although the limits of textual publishing may present few options for researchers. Including photographs may be possible, although these will typically only be published in black and white; some publishers will allow color images to be used, but only on Web versions of publications, and often with a fee charged to the author. Researchers need to select images carefully to ensure appropriate reproduction in black and white, particularly when screen captures are used from video files, where the resolution may be quite poor. Printing a copy of the article will give the researcher a feel for what a reader might experience by showing how the images will translate into black-and-white printed formats. Although some online journals do allow researchers to upload audio files or other materials to supplement the written article, these remain few in number.

It is important to consider how multimedia texts may be used for dissemination when the project is being designed. This will allow researchers to gather materials in appropriate data formats (e.g., high-resolution photographs) for the venues to be targeted for publication. Also, it is important that the ethics application for the project include provisions for using participant-generated materials (such as artwork created during an interview) or documents where participants are identified (such as photographs or audio recordings), so that these can be included in conference presentations, workshops, research reports, and other outputs. Where copyrighted materials are used in the project (such as website interfaces or archival photographs), researchers will also need to seek permission to use these materials in publications resulting from the research. In some cases, the copyright holder may allow for such use with the addition of a permission statement; in others, a fee may be required for use, particularly in publications that generate revenue.

More questions? See #66, #68, and #99.

Journal Articles in My Discipline Are Limited in Length, So How Can I Present My Results in a Succinct Way While Providing Enough Detail to Support My Arguments?

Journal articles vary in the length that publishers will accept, with longer articles being more common in the humanities and social sciences. Journals that typically publish quantitative research may also have shorter publishing guidelines than those that publish qualitative research or a mix of paradigms. It is important to review the guidelines when first selecting a journal to be aware of these limitations; however, it is also worth asking the editor if longer articles will be accepted, or if it is possible to publish two companion articles (part "a" and part "b") to present a more complete account of the results.

In general, qualitative articles require more space to be able to provide the depth of evidence required by the analysis. Lengthy participant quotes and detailed excerpts of texts, for example, are expected of qualitative writing practices, and typically demand a longer word count (i.e., 5,000+ words) to present a complete picture of the analysis with appropriate evidence. However, much will depend on the scope of the topic being presented. Where a chosen journal has a very limited word count (i.e., up to 2,000 words), a researcher may need to focus on a single theme of the analysis, rather than attempting to link multiple themes together. Even where the publication limits are longer, a researcher may choose to focus on a single theme in depth, providing more evidence or with additional theoretical explorations in the analysis. Of course, ensuring that writing is clear, concise, and succinct will allow researchers to maximize the available word count. Ensuring that the literature review and research design sections are concise, for example, will provide more room for the results and discussion to be presented. In all cases, brevity must be balanced with the provision of rich examples drawn from the dataset as evidence for the claims made. As the goal of qualitative writing is to "give voice" to participants' experiences, publications must provide detailed quotes from participants, rather than short summaries or paraphrasing by the researchers alone to meet word count limits.

Typically, qualitative research projects generate several publications, rather than a single report of results. Even in a PhD dissertation, a student may not present all of the relevant themes to the level of detail that the data analysis could allow; the student will tend to focus on major themes, presenting those in depth, and leaving other, minor themes for future analysis and publication. Researchers need to develop publication plans where they list the themes to be addressed and name the targeted venues for those publications (including word limitations). Specific points of evidence should be divided across the publications to ensure (for example) that quotes are not repeated and that data are drawn from across all participants. By planning the publication set in advance, and targeting more detailed themes to journals with longer word count provisions, researchers can ensure that the data will be treated with the depth and attention required of qualitative writing while meeting the practical needs of editors and publishers.

More questions? See #66, #91, and #93.

I Have a Lot of Data and I'm Struggling to Fit Everything Into One Paper! How Can I Write Up My Results in a Single Research Report?

One of the joys of qualitative research is the amount of deep, rich data that emerges from data collection. In projects involving triangulation in particular, researchers may have hundreds of pages of transcripts, hours of video recordings, and journals filled with participants' reflections. Typically, researchers do not publish results in a single research report. Even a doctoral dissertation project, which is designed to present the results of a significant, multiyear project, will often present only a selection of findings from the full dataset. Although this can seem overwhelming, the benefit of this type of work is that it can be mined for several months—if not years—due to the nature of the data gathered.

Researchers should put a publication plan together at the point of data collection and analysis. It may be possible to divide the dataset by method, for example, where focus group data, observational data, and interview data are published separately. However, it is more common in qualitative writing to divide the content into a series of thematic pieces, whether these are journal articles, book chapters, conference papers and so on. In this case, a researcher will consider the themes that are emerging from the analysis and craft a publication plan where the various themes can be addressed, drawing evidence from across the various methods used in a study. This approach allows the benefits of triangulation to shine through, as the reader can see the specific theme from a variety of angles. For example, a study of bullying in high school may explore the concept of "resilience," drawing data from interviews with teens, postings to social media, and focus groups with teachers. In this way, the researcher can present a deeper analysis of the concept of "resilience" than could be done if the datasets were divided by each method and reviewed separately.

In this way, researchers can mine their datasets for a variety of themes, publishing their work over several months and targeting various, relevant publications. If a researcher wants to publish a book on his or her core findings, he or she may choose a number of related or complementary themes to inform this lengthier publication, while keeping other, discrete findings for publication in journal form. Seeking advice from colleagues and community partners can guide the process of theme selection, as there may be strategic reasons to choose specific topics to publish at specific times. An open call for book chapters, for example, may provide a good opportunity for a researcher to share his or her work, even if the theme is not one she or he may have otherwise prioritized. Similarly, a researcher may want to publish papers on specific themes to be able to point to the findings in a grant application on a related topic. Although the publication plan is an important step in prioritizing thematic publications, the plan should be flexible enough to allow for unanticipated publication opportunities as well.

More questions? See #39, #66, and #95.

Qualitative Research Reports Are Published in Many Formats and Styles, Ranging From Traditional (i.e., With Results, Discussion, and Conclusions) to Progressive (e.g., Narrative Short Stories, Poetry, Plays). Which Approach Should I Choose for My Own Report?

Decisions about writing style need to be made in the context of the norms of the research discipline, the venue chosen for publication, and the nature of the project itself. In disciplines where qualitative research is prevalent (such as sociology and education), innovative writing practices may be very welcome. In disciplines where quantitative approaches are the norm (such as medicine and engineering), qualitative researchers may rely on traditional styles of writing. Reputable publishing venues within the discipline provide guidance to researchers on what is typical for that field. A traditional journal, for example, may specify that articles include particular headings in a particular order (such as introduction, literature review, research design, results, discussion, conclusions). Progressive journals may allow researchers to use their own headings and organizational structure. Author guidelines provided on the publishers' websites outline specific rules and limitations.

In terms of content, researchers should review a sample of published work in their venue of choice to see what is acceptable for the audience of that journal. Reviewing these documents will clarify expectations related to the overall tone of the piece, the use of third versus first person, the inclusion of creative elements in the analysis (such as poetry), the addition of multimedia elements in online publications, and other elements of writing style. Certainly, publishing venues also change over time, particularly when new editors are involved, so it is important to review content on a regular basis to get a feel for how best to structure a research report.

One of the most common tensions qualitative researchers face in writing research reports is when they wish to publish in a particular, top-tier venue in the discipline only to find that the publication guidelines are not conducive to qualitative writing. Qualitative reports are typically longer than quantitative reports, for example, due to the need to include participant quotes in the presentation of the evidence. Similarly, as the results and discussion are typically integrated in qualitative writing, journals requiring that publications have separate "results" and "discussion" sections are not appropriate for qualitative projects. Some researchers may decide to write in more traditional ways in order to publish in their chosen venue; others may decide to choose another venue, which will be more accepting of qualitative writing styles. Another alternative is to contact the editor to discuss how best to alter the guidelines to suit the needs of the qualitative project. Whatever the choice, it is important that researchers stay true to the nature of their qualitative approach and choose a venue that will support the writing style they need to reflect in their work.

More questions? See #2, #94, and #96.

What Kind of Audience Reads Qualitative Research Reports, Typically?

Qualitative research is read by people in many different roles and organizational contexts, as well as at various stages of their careers. Certainly, academic audiences (from students to professors) read qualitative research reports regularly. Qualitative researchers often have these groups in mind when they are writing their research reports, particularly when writing for journals, books, and other academic venues. However, researchers should remember that readers might be at different stages of their career or come from very different disciplines than those of the authors. Writing in an accessible way, to the "unknown but educated reader," is usually a good practice in most academic writing. However, seeking advice from colleagues, especially when conducting interdisciplinary research, is a useful starting place to ensure that the chosen venue will target key academics who may benefit from reading the research results.

Outside of academe, readers of qualitative research include government officials (such as policymakers), practitioners (such as teachers, nurses, and engineers), industry representatives (such as pharmaceutical companies), and research participants. Where researchers believe that particular nonacademic audiences will benefit from knowing about the results directly, the research team may target specific reports to reach these groups. Articles in industry trade journals, reports in practice-oriented journals and magazines, or submissions to community newsletters are just a few of the ways that researchers share their results with nonacademic audiences. However, it is important to note that different audiences require different writing styles so the work is accessible and relevant to that group. Consideration must be given to writing style, reading level, venue, and other details to ensure that the target group will be able to see and understand the results being presented. Seeking advice from members of the target group about the best way to reach key stakeholders may be the best starting place for most researchers.

More questions? See #2, #11, and #91.

My Data Are Just Interview Transcripts and Other Texts, So How Can I Present My Findings in a Visual Poster Presentation?

Many academic disciplines include poster presentations as part of their conference events, where scholars can provide details on the study design, as well as project findings. Qualitative researchers often find these posters to be challenging to design, given the focus on textual data (such as interview transcripts) in project designs. Researchers need to think carefully and creatively about the design of these types of research posters to ensure that the presentation of findings is as strong as it can be. Well-designed posters

- **Follow the published guidelines.** Conference organizers will provide details on the size and orientation of the poster, as well as any specific design principles that must be followed. Whether the poster will be pinned to a wall or resting on an easel will affect your chosen design.
- **Break the text into readable sections.** Readers will scan your poster, rather than reading everything word for word. Using numbered lists, bullets, and other strategies to break the text into sections will guide people through your poster.
- **Use font size, color, and white space appropriately.** Where text is provided, be sure to leave enough white space—and a large font size—so the poster can be read easily from a distance. Most readers will stand a few feet away from the poster, especially in a crowded space. Providing brief quotes on the poster that are in a different font color, or in bold, can add a visual element to the design that will catch the reader's eye.
- **Include images.** This is a visual medium, so including images, graphs, drawings, and so on, is essential. Consider what images will best represent your participant group, setting, or topic; search for free images online or purchase stock photos to use as part of your

design. Original artwork (created by the research team or by participants) can also enhance your design.

- **Acknowledge the institution, funding agencies, research partners, and so on.** Be sure to include institutional logos, names of groups providing funding, names of partner organizations, and others involved in the project (such as research assistants). You may need to obtain permission to include logos or to name certain individuals/organizations, so be sure to plan ahead on the design to allow time for these approvals to be given.

- **Accompany with handouts, business cards, or other "take-aways."** Not all details need to be included on the poster itself. Many researchers provide handouts to presentation attendees, such as reference lists. They also give out business cards so that they do not need to provide full contact details on the poster. A small, print copy of the poster to give to interested readers is another way to ensure that people remember the work after the conference ends and can get in touch with the team if they want more details.

More questions? See #2, #68, and, #91.

Should I Send Copies of My Publications to My Participants?

Many qualitative researchers share the results of their projects with their participants. When participants are involved as partners or co-investigators in the research, they may be involved in data analysis and writing; they may be named as co-authors on a publication or listed in the acknowledgements, depending on their role in the project. In other cases, community partners may be provided with a report summarizing key findings of the project. This approach may be preferable to providing copies of academic publications (such as journal articles), as specialized reports can target specific issues and implications for the community group that has been involved in the project. Some qualitative researchers also opt to share results in other forms (such as through seminars, workshops, articles in community newsletters, etc.). These strategies also allow researchers to target their writing or presentation style to the community group's needs directly. Typically, reporting results to the community will be a requirement of the partnership between the groups, so planning a strategy for sharing results is an important part of the study design.

In qualitative projects where the participants are not involved directly in the design and implementation of the research, it is common to offer to share publications of key findings with participants. Often, this is used as a way to say "thank you" to participants, who may have given freely of their time to be part of the research. In these cases, qualitative researchers will need to keep an archive of contact details for participants so that they can share the project outcomes at a later date; this must also be addressed in the original ethics application for the project. However, as there can be several weeks, months, or even years before project results are published (depending on the study design), researchers often find it preferable to create a brief summary of findings that they can share with participants soon after the project has ended. These documents can be targeted to the needs of the participant group, in terms of writing style and implications for practice; updated versions can also be shared at later dates, with citations provided to formal publications for those participants who want to learn more. Researchers also may provide details on a public website where participants (and other interested individuals) can follow the project as it proceeds. This strategy can be useful, in particular, as researchers do not need to track participants over the long term.

More questions? See #10, #11, and #83.

Index

SAGE researchmethod

The essential online tool for researchers from world's leading methods publisher

Find exactly what you are looking for, from basic explanations to advanced discussion

More content and new features added this year!

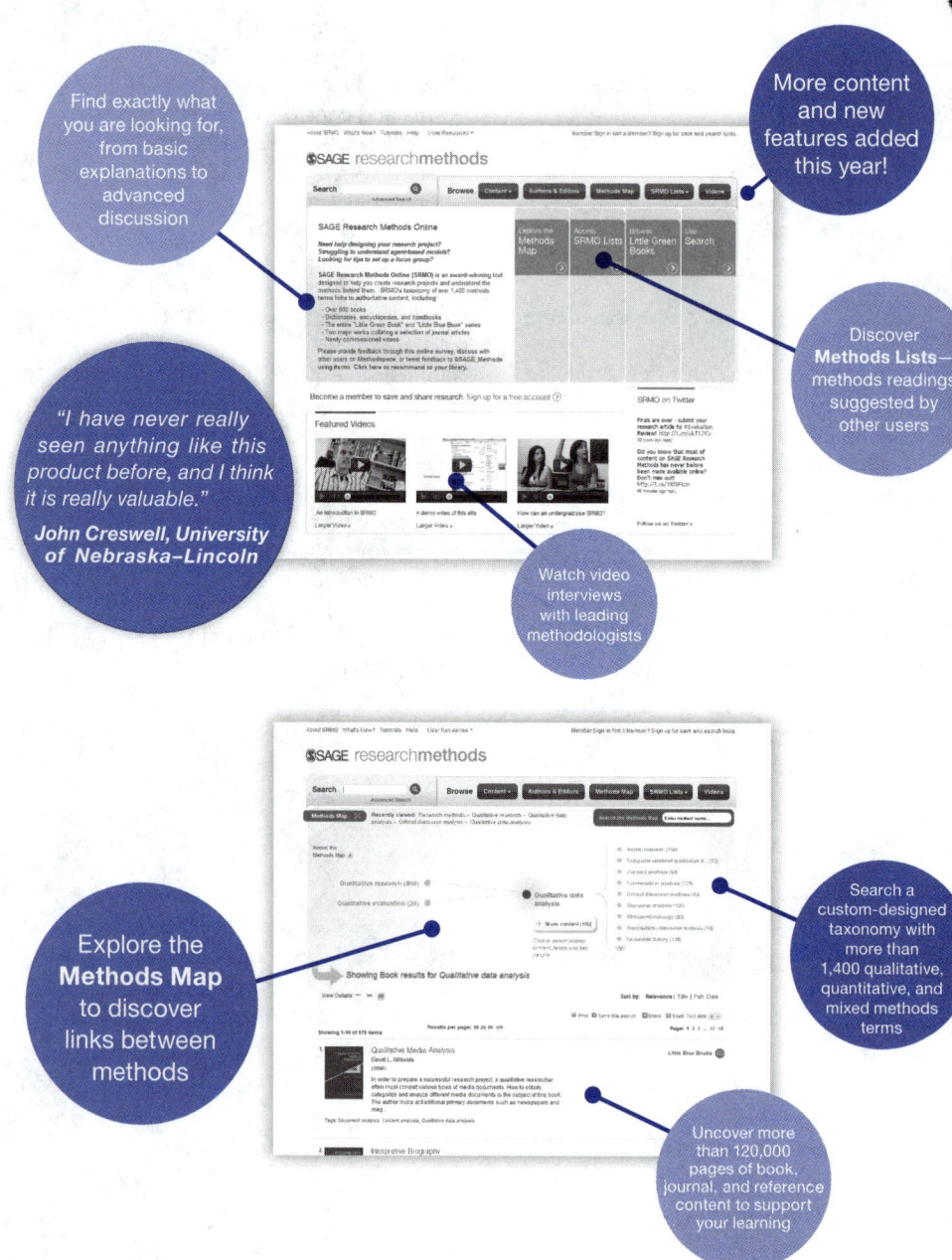

Discover **Methods Lists**— methods readings suggested by other users

"I have never really seen anything like this product before, and I think it is really valuable."

John Creswell, University of Nebraska–Lincoln

Watch video interviews with leading methodologists

Explore the **Methods Map** to discover links between methods

Search a custom-designed taxonomy with more than 1,400 qualitative, quantitative, and mixed methods terms

Uncover more than 120,000 pages of book, journal, and reference content to support your learning

Find out more at
www.sageresearchmethods.com